Crafting an Asian Future in the Post-COVID-19 Asia

Highly Recommended Titles

Impact of COVID-19 on Asian Economies and Policy Responses
edited by Sumit Agarwal, Zhiguo He and Bernard Yeung
ISBN: 978-981-122-937-4

Post-COVID Asia: Deglobalization, Fourth Industrial Revolution, and Sustainable Development
by Hyun-Hoon Lee and Donghyun Park
ISBN: 978-981-122-897-1
ISBN: 978-981-123-023-3 (pbk)

Revitalising ASEAN Economies in a Post-COVID-19 World: Socioeconomic Issues in the New Normal
edited by Hooi Hooi Lean
ISBN: 978-981-122-846-9

Crafting an Asian Future in the Post-COVID-19 Asia

Edited by

Tai Wei Lim
Soka University, Japan

World Scientific

NEW JERSEY • LONDON • SINGAPORE • BEIJING • SHANGHAI • HONG KONG • TAIPEI • CHENNAI • TOKYO

Published by

World Scientific Publishing Co. Pte. Ltd.
5 Toh Tuck Link, Singapore 596224
USA office: 27 Warren Street, Suite 401-402, Hackensack, NJ 07601
UK office: 57 Shelton Street, Covent Garden, London WC2H 9HE

Library of Congress Cataloging-in-Publication Data
Names: Lim, Tai-Wei, editor.
Title: Crafting an Asian future in the post-COVID-19 Asia /
edited by Tai Wei Lim, Soka University, Japan.
Description: New Jersey : World Scientific, [2023]
Identifiers: LCCN 2022022558 | ISBN 9789811253720 (hardcover) |
ISBN 9789811253737 (ebook) | ISBN 9789811253744 (ebook other)
Subjects: LCSH: Asia--Economic conditions--21st century. | Asia--Social conditions--
21st century. | COVID-19 Pandemic, 2020---Economic aspects--Asia. |
COVID-19 Pandemic, 2020---Social aspects--Asia.
Classification: LCC HC412 .C73 2023 | DDC 330.95--dc23/eng/20220512
LC record available at https://lccn.loc.gov/2022022558

British Library Cataloguing-in-Publication Data
A catalogue record for this book is available from the British Library.

For any available supplementary material, please visit
https://www.worldscientific.com/worldscibooks/10.1142/12763#t=suppl

Desk Editors: Nimal Koliyat/Lixi Dong

Typeset by Stallion Press
Email: enquiries@stallionpress.com

https://doi.org/10.1142/9789811253737_fmatter

Foreword: Uncertain Future Prospects in the Post-COVID-19 World

It is impossible to evaluate with certainty how much the world has been transformed by the COVID-19 pandemic. Scientists, economists, politicians, and the public are increasingly concerned about the evolution of COVID-19 over time of the pandemic. The transformative powers of COVID-19 have affected almost all aspects of contemporary social life. In the post-COVID-19 world, how will the major dimensions of everyday life (economics, politics, culture, ideology, etc.) look like? How have specific industries, stakeholders, and regions "suffered" or "benefited" from this unprecedented time? This book provides a transdisciplinary approach to discussing various related topics. Fundamentally, there are at least three key questions to be answered in the post-COVID-19 world.

First, is the age of globalization over? Market globalists firmly believe that globalization is inevitable and irreversible. Since the end of the Cold War, the geopolitical conditions appear to have dissipated and the world has nearly triumphed in the liberalization and integration of markets. Before the appearance of COVID-19, few could foresee that the world would become less interdependent. Yet, the internationalization of trade in goods and services has been greatly interrupted by the pandemic. The COVID-19 pandemic has had a negative impact on global foreign direct investments (FDIs) flows.[1] Global tourism has also fallen sharply

[1] "Impact of the COVID-19 Pandemic on Trade and Development: Transitioning to A New Normal," United Nations Conference on Trade and Development, 2020, Chapter 1,

and global economies have plummeted since 2020. Apparently, the impact of COVID-19 on global economic growth and international trade has been greater than the 2008 Global Financial Crisis and the recent US–China trade disputes combined. While globalization is generally synonymous with the process of time-space compression, it is ironic to witness that the world has rapidly disconnected in the era of globalization. Furthermore, we can examine the powers and the role of governments in the "self-regulating" market for a global order in the future. Under which circumstances can civic campaigns and organizations assist national or transnational governments to generate a joint approach to combating the coronavirus pandemic? If not, can we conclude that globalization and liberal global governance are simply myths and illusions?

Second, will there be a rise of new great powers in the post-COVID world? Since the 2010s, there have been an increasing number of writings on the emergence of China and Asia's rise in the 21st century. Various Asian countries and regions adopted different approaches to combating the COVID-19 pandemic. However, it seems complicated to measure outcomes in the fight against the coronavirus. If we define power as the ability to attract followers and set the agenda for international negotiations, it is hard to pick a few superpowers that can build a consensus and a coordinated global effort. Religious debate regarding COVID-19 is another important issue. In the post-Cold War era, it was argued that the world order has been influenced by the clash of major world civilizations. Conservatives, hawks, and realists consolidated and propagated this belief, especially after the 11 September 2001 attacks. How religious leaders interact with political leaders and scientists in the fight against the coronavirus not only advances their power, norms, and values but also affects the personal and collective identities of billions of people.

Perhaps there have been more heated debates over the "live with the virus" or partial/complete lockdown approaches in the process of combating the COVID-19 coronavirus. Social distancing and other pandemic-related measures have elicited a large amount of public anxiety and anger in many regions. To a certain extent, the anxiety or a negative state of mind has also been aggravated by anti-Chinese feeling/sentiments across the world. These people are unhappy with the Chinese-style tight restrictions which apparently violate individual freedom. In some places, people

available at https://unctad.org/system/files/official-document/osg2020d1_en.pdf, last updated on 6 February 2022.

opted to avoid Chinese restaurants whereas others even abused Chinese people in verbal and physical attacks. It was unsurprising to know that Chinese or even Asian communities have become a target in many regions. How the COVID-19 pandemic will affect racial prejudice toward Chinese people in advanced economies and Belt and Road countries is another important topic especially in the study of the rise of China.

Last, global inequality is always a problem. It is important to examine the relationship between advanced and developing economies in the post-COVID-19 world. Some countries such as Iran suffered severely as the country faced restrictions to purchase COVID vaccines and basic medical equipment. This structural division is a consequence of economic development in the pre-COVID-19 era. Possibly, the world will be generally divided into vaccinated and unvaccinated once global economies restart. Global inequality and poverty will continue to grow without an effective reform of global institutions.

Still, there are numerous problems ahead in the post-COVID world. For example, the explosion of science and technology in the 19th century intensified global interconnections in the 20th century. Will it be a beginning of a new digital world when everyone gets used to the web in the post-COVID-19 era? How will the world be united together? The post-COVID-19 world leaves even more questions for us to discover in the future. I believe that this edited volume can enlighten us on the possibilities of our future from different perspectives.

Wing Lok Hung
China Economic Research Programme
Lingnan University, Hong Kong SAR

https://doi.org/10.1142/9789811253737_fmatter

About the Editor

Tai Wei Lim is a professional historian and area studies specialist, focusing on Northeast Asia, especially Chinese and Japanese studies.

https://doi.org/10.1142/9789811253737_fmatter

About the Contributors

Elim Wong obtained her Ph.D. in Japanese Studies from The Chinese University of Hong Kong. Her major research interest is on Chinese diaspora in Japan with major focus on Chinese folk religion, and she is also interested in East Asia popular culture and history.

Ka Shing Ng is Associate Professor in the Faculty of Humanities and Human Sciences at Hokkaido University. He is a sociologist by training and an area study specialist on contemporary China and Japan. His research interests lie primarily in social movements in East Asia and the sociology of culture and religion. He has written and published extensively in Japanese and English. His most recent publications have appeared in *Religions*, *Social Transformations in Chinese Societies*, and *Japan–China Journal of Sociological Studies*.

Samantha Ka Mei Ma is a solicitor practicing in Hong Kong with a Ph.D. in International Relations from the University of Sheffield. She is also an adjunct Assistant Professor in the Department of Japanese Studies at the Chinese University of Hong Kong, teaching the course of International Relations of Japan. She graduated with a Bachelor of Laws from University of Hong Kong, Master of Laws in Chinese Law (with Distinction) in City University of Hong Kong, and Master of Arts in Japanese Studies from the Chinese University of Hong Kong. She is also a fellow of the Chartered Institute of Arbitrators. Her research interests lie in Hong Kong law, PRC law, and the international relations of East Asia. As a solicitor in Hong Kong, she is also a member of the Council for the Promotion of Guangdong–Hong Kong–Macau Cooperation which helps promote the legal and academic exchanges across the legal community in Hong Kong, Macau and Guangdong.

Satoshi Abe is Assistant Professor in the Graduate School of Integrated Sciences for Global Society at Kyushu University, Japan. He is a cultural anthropologist working on diverse subjects related to modernity, science, and religion in Asia with a particular focus on Iran, where he has conducted ethnographic field research since 2009. His publications include *Pursuing Moral Dimensions of the Environment: A Study of Islamic Tradition in Contemporary Iran* and *Conceptions of Nature in Iran: Science, Nationalism, and Heteroglossia*.

Wilson Lee is an assistant instructor at the Lingnan University and a teaching assistant at the Chinese University of Hong Kong, and had the opportunity to offer courses at higher diploma and undergraduate level, ranging from East Asian history and culture to modern and contemporary Japanese society. Lee received positive feedback from students, particularly of the courses Japan History and the

History of Sino-Japanese Relations and Japanese Popular Culture, who comment the comparative approach Lee deploys is one of the inspirations for their learning. Lee's research interest in East Asian history can be complementary to the teaching. His projects include the impact of "learning from Japan" to East Asia in the 1970s and 1980s, and he is also interested in studying historical development in East Asia from a comparative perspective. Hong Kong and Singapore, for example, are two of the research subjects in his Ph.D. dissertation to understand the impact of "learning from Japan" in East Asian societies through comparison. Hence, the ongoing and future research do not only enrich courses contents from time to time but also inspires Lee to draft other potential courses in the future. Lee teaches a range of courses from history to cultural studies at undergraduate and postgraduate levels. In the field of history, for example, Lee can offer courses such as the history of Japan, the history of China, the history of Hong Kong, and East Asian history since the modern era. In the field of popular culture, Lee has experience in offering a course of Japanese popular culture, and he is also able to teach courses like the cultural flow in East Asia.

Wing Lok Hung obtained his Ph.D. in International Relations from Tsinghua University, China, and is now working for the China Economic Research Programme at Lingnan University, Hong Kong SAR. After completing his bachelor's studies in Government and Public Administration from the Chinese University of Hong Kong in 2009, he continues to receive education from institutes in the United Kingdom, the Netherlands, and Beijing China. Occasionally, he delivers preliminary observations and analysis on various topics related to China and the global political economy, as well as domestic issues in Hong Kong. His articles have appeared in a wide range of journals and newspapers, including *Asian Education and Development Studies*, *China and the World: Ancient and Modern Silk Road*, *Hong Kong and Macao Journal*, *Hong Kong Economic Journal*, *Singtao Daily*, *Takungpao*, and *Hong Kong Commercial Daily*.

Wong Chong Wai, Kenneth, PBM graduated from the National University of Singapore in 2011 with a Degree in Social Work. In 2016, Kenneth completed his Master's in Community Leadership and Social Development with Singapore University of Social Sciences. Kenneth is currently a Lecturer with the Institute of Technical Education, lecturing the Work-Study Diploma in Community Engagement and Development. Kenneth spent most of his time on grassroots and community work, engaging with residents on various social issues. In recognition of his service to the community, Kenneth was conferred the National Day Award 2017 — Public Service Medal (Pingat Bakti Masyarakat).

Yoshihisa Godo received his Ph.D. degree from the University of Kyoto in 1992. His areas of research include development economics and agricultural economics. His *Development Economics* (3rd edition), co-authored with Yujiro Hayami and published by the Oxford University Press in 2005, is especially well known. His book written in Japanese, *Nihon no Shoku to Nou* (Food and Agriculture in Japan), received the 28th Suntory Book Prize in 2006, which is one of the most prestigious academic book prizes in Japan. He is also engaged in various social activities such as the Special Councillor to the Osaka City Government. He participates in the International Zheng He Society as an associate member as well as an honorary advisor.

https://doi.org/10.1142/9789811253737_fmatter

Contents

https://doi.org/10.1142/9789811253737_0001

Chapter 1

Introduction

Tai Wei Lim

Not too long ago, the world was busy crafting a global future with unmitigated globalization and the relentless march of Industry 4.0. A black swan event then happened. An outbreak of COVID-19 coronavirus surged through the world and resulted in a global pandemic that devastated economies, eliminated the weak/infirmed/elderly/young, and then targeted the general population. It devastated small and medium-sized enterprises (SMEs) and hastened the demise of sunset industries, resulting in record numbers of bankruptcies. This review volume had its origins in such unprecedented devastation. But, instead of succumbing to the despair of a worldwide cataclysmic event, a group of scholars from multiple disciplines got together, determined to turn the crisis into an opportunity by collaborating across borders and communicating through electronic means to put this publication together and also organizing a panel for one of the world's largest Asian scholarly conferences. Through sheer determination not to be hindered by a worldwide event, this group of scholars put their different specialization to use and adopted an on-site viewpoint of how the pandemic affected their lives and also the lives of the communities in their studies.

One of the industries that the pandemic era has highlighted is the importance of the agricultural sector. This publication is honored to have a Suntory field prize award-winning professor, a towering academic in the field of agricultural economies in Japan to explain to the readers the impact of the COVID-19 coronavirus pandemic on the agricultural sector.

While the economic impact (as in the Main Street and Wall Street economies) is intensely discussed in terms of the impact from the pandemic, there is, however, a de-privileged emphasis on its impact on the agricultural industry. Here is where Y. Godo picks up and goes in-depth in his observations and studies of farming sectors and communities affected by the pandemic in Japan. This is an important chapter as the country case study of Japan provides a look into how a country that was unable to lock down due to post-war constitutional constraints and even had to organize the largest sporting event in the world (the postponed 2021 Summer Olympics) coped with the outbreak. In particular, given Godo's expertise, he examined the country's agricultural sector in particular.

Godo approached the topical matter from a systemic level. He noted that Japan has established a unique agricultural cooperative system called Nokyo. As Japan's largest agricultural group, Nokyo had been extensively involved in both economic and political activities until the early 1990s. It also held a leading position in the agricultural political dynamics; further, it successfully organized farmers and inspired consumers to support the Japanese government's agricultural protection policy. For example, in the trade negotiations of the Uruguay Round of the General Agreement on Tariffs and Trade (1988–1994), Nokyo formulated a strong political campaign against Japan opening its rice market. However, Japan's election and financial reforms in the middle of the 1990s undermined Nokyo's political power. Currently, it seems appropriate for Nokyo to adopt the principles of cooperative movements that advocate political neutrality.

In his second provocative chapter titled "The End of the Agriculture Boom in Japan under the COVID-19 Pandemic," Godo tackles an even more longitudinal and macro subject matter which is a critique of the agricultural system. In doing so, he is provoking the readers to critically examine what he considers as challenges faced by the sector in the context of a pandemic and Godo tries to overturn conventional thinking in this controversial chapter. The readers may not agree with his assessment but Godo traces his chapter on perceptions to the first decade of the 21st century. Following the 2008 global financial crisis, the social phenomenon of the trend of dreaming about agriculture, christened the "agriculture boom," began in 2009. Losing the national pride of being the second largest economy in the world and the economic leader of Asian countries, the Japanese general public wanted to forget this unpleasant reality by making up rosy (but empty) stories about Japanese agriculture.

In addition, Godo opines that Japanese manufacturers were motivated to start new businesses related to farming. While the agricultural boom picked up among the general public and manufacturers, it did not stem from the reality of Japanese agriculture. The COVID-19 pandemic exposed the vulnerability of agriculture in Japan to the public; it became apparent that Japanese agriculture would be unable to survive without foreign tourists' strong and significant demand for Japanese agricultural products, and without the foreign laborers employed in Japanese farms. Consequently, the Japanese's preoccupation with agriculture was dampened after the outbreak of COVID-19. In addition, the economic impact and turmoil of this pandemic necessitated that Japanese manufacturers turn their attention to their primary businesses (instead of starting new businesses related to farming). Therefore, that the Japanese agricultural boom is now dying out is Godo's controversial proposition.

Besides specific-sector industries like agriculture, the pandemic added on to anti-globalization forces as it disrupted supply chains, physical connectivity, eliminated much of the hospitality and service retail industry (Wong and Lee's chapter on Yokohama Chinatown is a micro-study), and threatened to devastate the service industry. Historically, Yokohama Chinatown had encountered other apocalyptic events. Just like coronavirus is a natural phenomenon (at the point of this writing, most scientists established that the COVID-19 coronavirus is not a lab-made pathogen), another kind of disaster in the form of a massive apocalyptic earthquake also hit the Chinatown in 1923. The year 2020 turned out to be a very challenging year for everyone. Japan and the world were struck by the COVID-19 coronavirus pandemic which caught the world by surprise starting from 23 January 2020 when it was publicly revealed by the Chinese authorities. Tourists headed for the Chinatown declined in numbers as early as January 2020 when Japan confirmed its first COVID-19 infection.

Wong and Lee noted that this was made worse by fake news that the infected individual was from the Chinatown and, by March 2020, some eateries in the Chinatown received racially charged messages attributing the outbreak to Chinese individuals and demanded them to get out of Japan soon. Yokohama Chinatown restaurateurs sought solidarity with other nearby premium establishments to cope with the economic impact of COVID-19 coronavirus pandemic. In solidarity with other external retailers to drawn tourists and visitors back, Yokohama Chinatown residents and their Japanese allies and stakeholders are working together to combat a common enemy — the economic impact of the COVID-19 coronavirus pandemic which does not differentiate between retailers or the prestige of the addresses.

Besides the economic impact on specific neighborhoods, the pandemic has also affected other stakeholders in a community like civil society groups. Ng analyzed this aspect in the case of Hong Kong's civil society. Hong Kong is one of the East Asian regional areas that has succeeded relatively well in containing the COVID-19 coronavirus pandemic in its early stages. While this can be partly attributed to the measures promptly implemented by the Hong Kong government, the role of its civil society in responding to the crisis should not be underestimated. Especially during the early outbreak, when the government was unable to solve the mask shortage problem effectively, many interested individuals and groups had taken the lead to secure mask supplies. This chapter examines the role of Hong Kong's civil society in the fight against the pandemic with a focus on the mask issue. It starts with an overview of the pandemic in Hong Kong and discusses some of the factors that have helped Hong Kong contain the outbreak as compared to other regions. By focusing on the mask shortage crisis during the early outbreak, Ng argues that one of the most important factors behind the so-called Hong Kong's "COVID-19 success story" (Leader League, 2020) is the resilience of Hong Kong's civil society. Due to travel restrictions, the author has not been able to conduct field studies in Hong Kong. Therefore, the data presented in this chapter were mainly based on textual materials collected online, such as news articles, government press releases, activity reports released by NGOs, etc.

Like Ng's chapter, Kenneth Wong's chapter also focuses on civil society pandemic mitigation efforts in the comparative case study of Singapore as a component of the country's all-of-society approach in combating the coronavirus. Leading the battle against COVID-19, Singapore government and various stakeholders in the community, through the Public, Private and People approach, rallied together to address the various social, health, financial challenges that arose in the pandemic. Wong's detailed chapter indicate to reader why Singapore has become a best practice example of COVID-19 mitigation as the state fully mobilizes its resources to help the country battle one of the world's deadliest crisis. Wong's chapter show how Singapore leaves no stones unturned in its quest to reach out to all members of society affected by the pandemic, including foreign workers, SMEs, and other vulnerable groups. The government's rapid response with budget relief has reinforced this collective response to the crisis. There is much to learn from the case study of Singapore in coping with the pandemic.

While some societal stakeholders like economic institutions and civil society groups try to cope with the changes wrought by the pandemic, other societies tackled more fundamental questions like the roles played by science and religion in their countries. Abe's case study on Iran is a par excellence writing on such fundamental contradictions. Abe expertly argues that religious debates about COVID-19 have generated a wide spectrum of Islamic viewpoints through which the crises of the pandemic are addressed and problematized, thus amplifying the religious frames of reference through which the pandemic is understood in the country. Given the historical and cultural significance of Islam in Iran, the discussions of public health management by the government are neither reducible to nor explicable by science alone. What religious perspectives and measures have emerged in Iran in a field that is predominantly conceptualized by scientific reasoning and scientific findings? In what ways are agreements and disagreements concerning public health measures addressed and debated among its religious leaders? What is the nature of the contention regarding the status of modern science among them? These are the questions this chapter seeks to address.

While the pandemic generated debates among stakeholders within a society like religious leaders and scientists, it harmed the retail service and agricultural sectors, affected civil society activities, truncated the process of globalization, and erected barriers to smooth trading relationships and even impacted on lifestyles but it hastened the utilization of technologies in our everyday lives, which is the subject of Lim's writing. Countries the world over have deployed their best possible capabilities such as advanced robotics, telemedicine, tracking systems, and big data analytics in their combat against the COVID-19 epidemic. Creative predictive models to project the spread and proliferation of the virus have been made possible by the use of algorithms, Artificial Intelligence (AI), and data analytics in analyzing big data. These sophisticated systems also represent tech capabilities and strengths of countries and carry implications for the tech sector post-COVID-19. Robots now work hand in hand with human operators who program them to clean up areas and deliver meals, beverages, and pharmaceuticals to people who need them while other categories of robots collect and supply data.

To prevent infected or potentially infected patients from turning up at clinics, community hospitals and polyclinics, doctors, health planners, and other stakeholders are using technologies to remotely connect these groups with doctors and medical practitioners to treat the patients from afar. However, there are also groups and individuals who are pushing back on such technological breakthroughs. The constant tensions between tech advocates and push-back resistance are likely to continue. Meanwhile, states are not waiting for tech skeptics to voice their complete support before they forge ahead with plans to create consortiums and partnerships of multiple tech systems to have a consolidated tech approach in battling the COVID-19 disease. The pandemic may stimulate many in medical establishments to change the way they practice medicine and reduce face-to-face consultations in the future, except for the most critical cases.

In moving fast to deal with the pandemic, some voices are urging restraints on the excesses of developments at warp speed, particularly with regard to the issue of privacy and personal rights issues. Samantha Ma covered a range of legal issues stemming from the COVID-19 pandemic in Hong Kong. There were voices of privacy concerns and discriminatory treatment of government healthcare measures. In the employment setting, the pandemic has brought severe financial hardships on businesses which in turn lead to change in employment rights and conditions of employees. There have also been a number of cases in which Hong Kong courts were invited to examine issues of the constitutionality of wearing masks and the impact of COVID-19 on the duration of tenancy agreements. Ma's chapter enlighten readers using case studies from Hong Kong related to rentals and leases and how it has thrown up unique legal issues that concerns public policy.

Finally, after detailing COVID-19 coronavirus pandemic's impacts on agriculture, local communities, and the sciences, it may be useful to wrap up the chapters with the final chapter before the conclusion on COVID-19's impact on global trade developments. Public policy related to privacy and health issues were not the only public policy items affected by the pandemic, trade policy from a macro interregional perspective is examined in this chapter, in particular, the pandemic's impact on the Belt and Road Initiative (BRI) as a case study. Despite the COVID-19 coronavirus pandemic, China appears to trudge ahead with its plans to develop the Maritime Silk Road (MSR) component of the BRI. This chapter by Tai Wei Lim will examine the impact of the pandemic on an ambitious interregional trade initiative. Moving from the BRI MSR region to a macro-global perspective, this chapter is accompanied by an updated chapter on the impact of Omicron on the global maritime trading network. The onset of Omicron infection came suddenly and without prior warning of its arrival. It caused great fear to shippers and logistics industry and many scrambled in the early days of Omicron, trying to cope with further disruptions as the world waited for data from South Africa to come in with regard to its severity. The anxiety was well understood by the logistical and shipping industry because their shipments had already been delayed even before the onset of Omicron. Many countries had their hands full dealing with the Delta infections. This challenge is discussed in the second last chapter before the conclusion.

Finally, against the context of the discussion on global trade in this section of the volume, the last word is given to HUNG, Wing-lok. He noted what only very few people would have imagined that our golden age of globalization would rapidly be obstructed in a similar way to what the forefathers experienced when WWII broke out and the Cold War that followed that disrupted globalization. In the contemporary case, the disintegration of the modern globalized world due to a worldwide spread of an infectious disease would also have been unimaginable to many. The COVID-19 pandemic is certainly a tipping point for globalization in the 21st century and invites comparison to a global phenomenon that defined the early 20th century: deglobalization. HUNG reflects on the impact of COVID-19 against the context of deglobalization, ending the volume's chapters on a self-reflective note on the pandemic's impact on global connectivity.

Overall, the volume content is interdisciplinary by nature and a product of exceptional contributions from a multidisciplinary panel of scholars, ranging from the anthropologist, sociologist, historians, and to economists. The interdisciplinary approach employed here allows one to critically look at and understand the subject matter — COVID-19 and its recovery — not just through diverse analytical frameworks but also through broader geographical (including Japan and Hong Kong), historical variations as well as technologies studies. There is no existing literature that is an exact equivalent on this subject matter given the ongoing pandemic as it unfolds simultaneously across regions and even continents, while exerting differential impacts on various sectors such as agriculture, religion, technology, etc. With the advantage of its interdisciplinary approaches examined in differing geographical locations, the volume makes a scholarly contribution to analyzing the COVID-19 pandemic outbreak that the coping mechanisms adopted by humankind in various capacities to mitigate it.

Part 1

COVID-19 and Agriculture

https://doi.org/10.1142/9789811253737_0002

Chapter 2

An Update on Japan's Agricultural Cooperatives in the Age of COVID-19

Yoshihisa Godo

Introduction

Japan's agricultural sector accounts for less than 1% of its national gross domestic product; however, this does not mean that agriculture is considered to be unimportant in Japanese politics. On the contrary, even the non-farmers in Japan closely follow agricultural issues, such as the Japanese government's agricultural trade negotiations. For years, Nokyo, Japan's unique agricultural cooperatives, played a pivotal role in agricultural political dynamics of the country. In particular, the National Central Union (NCU) functioned actively as Nokyo's political arm. The NCU kept an informal but close connection with the Liberal Democratic Party (LDP), which had been in power almost consistently since its establishment in 1955.

The NCU formulated its political agenda in consultation with farmers, organized demonstrations, and participated in the design and implementation of the government's agricultural programs. However, Nokyo's political power gradually weakened since the middle of the 1990s. In 2015, the LDP's administration deprived the NCU of its command over the Nokyo system. Nokyo's influence continued to wane in Japan's agricultural political dynamics. Why was Nokyo so politically powerful until the middle of the 1990s? Why has Nokyo's political power declined since then? This chapter aims to answer these questions and describe the changing role of Japan's agricultural cooperatives.

Traditional Structure of the Nokyo System

The NCU was established in 1954. This can be seen as the establishment of the traditional Nokyo system, which was maintained until 1997. The traditional Nokyo system has a three-tier structure, as can be seen in Figure 1.[1] Unit cooperatives in villages, towns, and cities constitute the first level. The unit cooperatives are in direct contact with farmers; each unit cooperative has its own jurisdiction and does not overlap with any other jurisdiction. Although there is no legal requirement, most farmers join Nokyo as regular members of the local unit cooperatives. Non-farm residents are also eligible to join unit cooperatives as associate members if they express sympathy with Nokyo and pay an entrance fee.[2] Both the regular and associate members are allowed to use any of the unit cooperatives' services, but only regular members are engaged in decision-making regarding their unit cooperative's activities. The president of a unit cooperative is elected from among regular members only (associate members do not have the right to vote and are not eligible for presidential election).

During the COVID-19 emergency, unit cooperatives sprung into action, rejuvenated by the needs to respond to a crisis. Unit cooperatives took actions in accordance with their Business Continuity Plans (BCPs), the state's Basic Response Policy and the prefectural response policies given that they are defined as "business requested to be continued" in state definitions (alongside the medical establishment, credit provision companies, cooperative insurance, production materials suppliers, agricultural

[1] The NCU was founded in 1954. This can be seen as the establishment of the traditional Nokyo system. Godo (2001) provides details of the traditional Nokyo system.

[2] Not only a farm household but also a legal person capitalized at 300 million yen or less who employs 300 individuals or less for farming is eligible to participate in local unit cooperatives as a regular member. Associate membership is open to any natural and legal persons (with no regulations on the size of the legal person or residential place) as long as they support Nokyo and pay entrance fees.

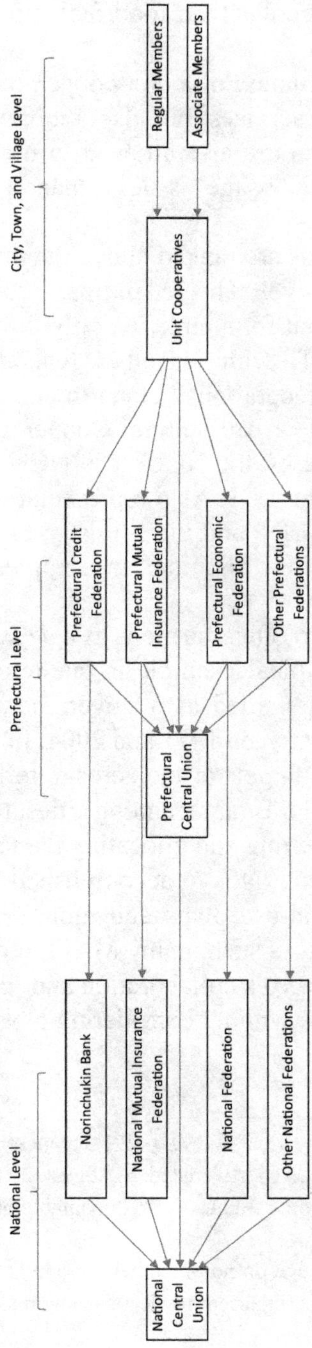

Figure 1. Nokyo's traditional three-tier structure.

feed, agricultural shippers/collectors, food/fuel suppliers, nurses, funeral parlors, etc.).[3]

Figure 2 shows the structure of a unit cooperative. Cooperatives provide not only agricultural services, but also almost every service related to daily life. Non-members are also allowed to use a unit cooperative's services as long as their usage is less than 15% of the services provided.[4]

Two tiers of federations are ranked above the unit cooperatives at the prefectural and national level. The federations provide similar services as the unit cooperatives, but for simplicity, only three types of federation are depicted in Figure 1, with all other federations being grouped together. The prefectural federations belong to and are supervised by the Prefectural Central Union of Agricultural Cooperatives and the national federations are supervised by the NCU. The NCU organizes farmers to form a voting group for the LDP. As a representative of the farmers, the NCU negotiates with the LDP and the Ministry of Agriculture, Forestry and Fisheries (MAFF) in designing and implementing agricultural policies.

Under the NCU, Nokyo often functions as a *de facto* sub-governmental body for the MAFF. A typical example is the acreage control program (ACP), which could be regarded as a government-led rice production cartel, that was effective between 1971 and 2004. In terms of the ACP, the MAFF first set a national target for the acreage to be diverted from rice planting and then allocated this target among cities, towns, and villages on a *pro rata* basis. In both setting and allocating the target, the MAFF considered the Nokyo's opinion. Nokyo accomplished the target acreage by drawing up local farmland-use plans and monitoring whether the rice farmers followed the plan. As such, many MAFF policies would not have been executed without Nokyo's collaboration and, therefore, the ministry does not introduce policies without considering Nokyo's opinion.

---

[3] Japan Co-operative Alliance, "(Beat COVID-19!) Japanese Cooperatives' Efforts to Combat COVID-19 (Summary Report)" dated 6 August 2020 in Japan Co-operative Alliance website [downloaded on 6 August 2020], available at https://www.japan.coop/wp/8110.

[4] The upper limit of the percentage on non-members' usage is higher than 15% in some types of businesses. For example, in accepting deposits and making loans, the upper limit is 20% instead of 15%.

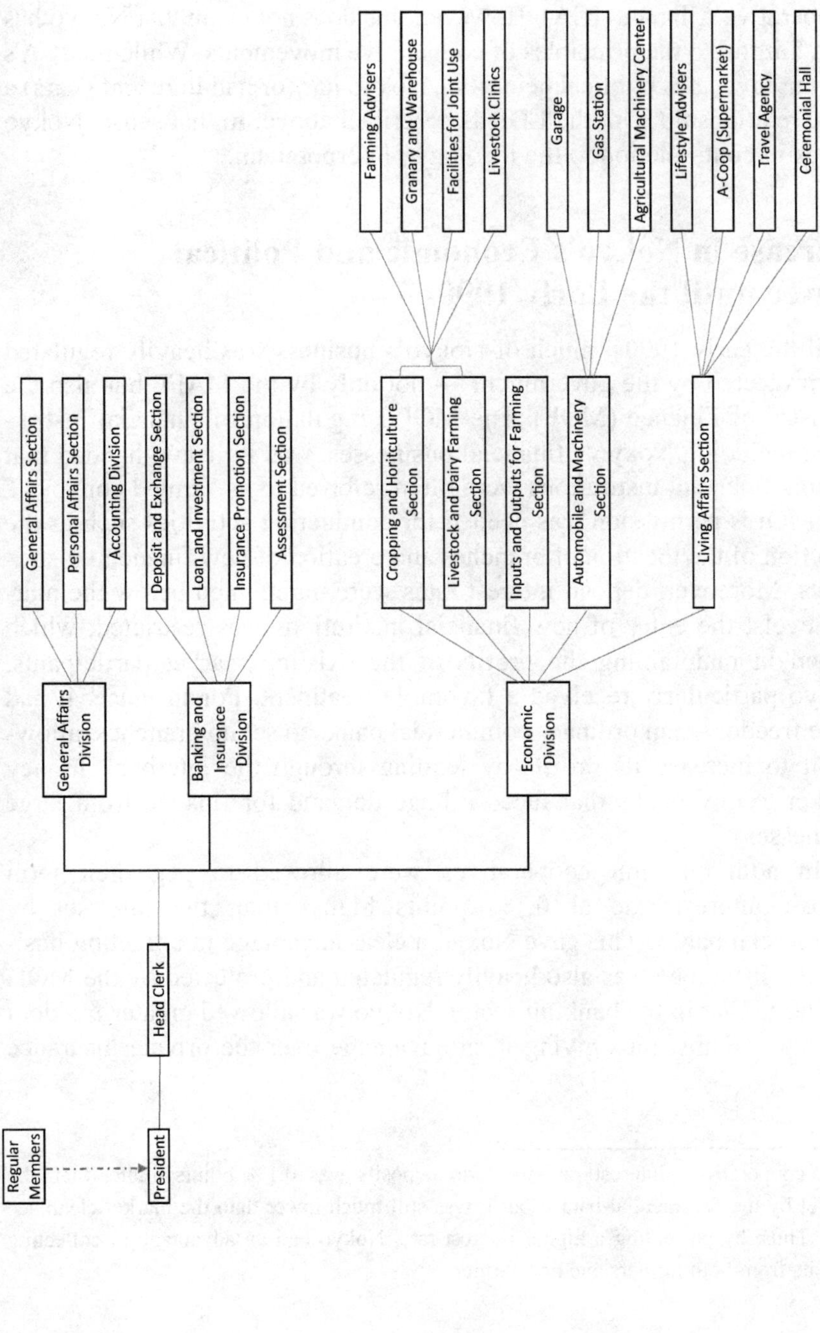

Figure 2. Model of a unit cooperative.

Nokyo is also active in networking with cooperatives throughout the world. For example, Nokyo is a prominent member of the International Cooperative Alliance (ICA). However, this does not mean that Nokyo has been faithful to the principles of cooperative movements. While the ICA's charter advocates political neutrality, Nokyo has (or had in recent years) a close relationship with the LDP as described above. In that sense, Nokyo stands in contradiction to the ideology of corporatism.

Increase in Nokyo's Economic and Political Power until the Early 1990s

Until the early 1990s, much of Nokyo's business was heavily regulated and protected by the government — not only by the MAFF but also the Ministry of Finance (MOF). The MOF's regulation of financial institutions, including Nokyo's financial businesses, was so heavy-handed that Japan's financial institutions were often referred to as "armed convoys." The MOF's permission was needed for conducting activities such as the selection of the location of branches and creation of new financial instruments. Moreover, deposit interest rates were maintained below the market levels; the entry of new financial institutions was restricted, which helped in maintaining the profits of the existing market participants. Nokyo particularly received a favorable treatment. For instance, it had more freedom than ordinary commercial banks to set up branches, allowing it to increase its profits by lending through the interbank money market to city banks that faced a huge demand for finance from large businesses.

In addition, unit cooperatives were allowed to peg their term deposit interest rate at 0.1% points higher than the rate set by commercial banks. This gave Nokyo a clear advantage in attracting businesses.[5] Insurance was also heavily regulated and protected by the MOF. Similar to that in the banking sector, Nokyo was allowed greater freedom to set premiums, thus giving it an advantage over the private insurance

---

[5]Unit cooperatives' interest rate for term deposits was 0.1% points higher than the rate set by the commercial banks, but it was still much lower than the market clearance level. Thus, by presenting a higher interest rate, Nokyo had an advantage in collecting deposits from both farmers and non-farmers.

companies.[6] The unit cooperatives themselves had (and still have) limited ability to manage their funds, and consigned these operations to the Prefectural Credit Federations, the Norinchukin Bank, the Prefectural Mutual Insurance Federations, and the National Mutual Insurance Federation.

As can be seen in column 4 of Table 1, most of the deposits that the unit cooperatives collected from households (including farm households) were (and still are to this day) redeposited into the upper federations. The profit margin between the redeposit interest rate and the deposit interest rate was relatively high until the early 1990s (column 8 of Table 1). Unit cooperatives obtained stable profits from commission charges by placing insurance funds into Prefectural Mutual Insurance Federations and the National Mutual Insurance Federation.

During the COVID-19 coronavirus pandemic, the Norinchukin Bank, JF Marine Bank (of the Fisheries Cooperative Group), and Rokin Banks dispensed low-interest loans, financial consultations, and facilitated repayments to buttress their members' livelihood and the health of the local economy while the Norinchukin Bank and JF Marine Bank set up an emergency fund to fight the COVID-19 coronavirus by offering low-interest loans and reduced guarantee fees for agriculturalists.[7] On 20 April 2020, the Rokin Banks initiated the "special unsecured loans to support the livelihood of workers affected by COVID-19" and, on 30 April 2020, they began taking up "special emergency small loans based on the situation caused by COVID-19 under the livelihood welfare fund system" applications managed by the Councils of Social Welfare.[8]

The presidents of the unit cooperatives, who were (and still are) respected leaders in the farming community, were (and still are) better politicians than the businesspeople. A lack in their business experience did not emerge as a significant barrier owing to the privileges generated by the banking and insurance businesses. The unit president simply set a target amount of deposits and insurance policies for all the staff. An example of such efforts was observed during the "deposit promotion

---

[6] For more details, see Saeki (1989).

[7] Japan Co-operative Alliance, "(Beat COVID-19!) Japanese Cooperatives' Efforts to Combat COVID-19 (Summary Report)" dated 6 August 2020 in Japan Co-operative Alliance website [downloaded on 6 August 2020], available at https://www.japan.coop/wp/8110.

[8] *Ibid.*

Table 1. Unit cooperatives' banking business.

Fiscal year	Balance of funds in banking at the fiscal year-end					Average interest rate on re-deposits in prefectural credit federations (6)	Average interest rate on deposits in unit cooperatives (7)	Profit margin (8) = (7) − (6)
	Deposits (1)	Re-deposits to prefectural credit federations (2)	Loans (3)	Re-deposits/ deposits (4) = (2)/(1)	Loans/ deposits (5) = (3)/(1)			
	billion yen					%		
1965	2,334	1,267	1,043	0.54	0.45	5.86	4.06	1.80
1966	2,838	1,499	1,281	0.53	0.45	5.58	4.02	1.57
1967	3,465	1,795	1,625	0.52	0.47	5.43	3.99	1.43
1968	4,086	2,062	1,984	0.50	0.49	5.52	4.04	1.48
1969	5,021	2,539	2,447	0.51	0.49	5.39	3.99	1.40
1970	5,934	2,887	3,008	0.49	0.51	5.76	4.16	1.60
1971	7,118	3,592	3,439	0.50	0.48	5.52	4.20	1.32
1972	9,238	4,947	3,995	0.54	0.43	5.18	3.94	1.24
1973	11,301	5,016	5,849	0.44	0.52	6.18	4.19	1.99
1974	12,993	5,536	6,850	0.43	0.53	6.81	5.20	1.61
1975	15,232	6,972	7,505	0.46	0.49	7.02	5.56	1.47
1976	17,303	8,405	8,178	0.49	0.47	6.67	5.23	1.44
1977	19,416	10,077	8,626	0.52	0.44	6.17	4.79	1.38
1978	21,906	12,224	8,794	0.56	0.40	5.05	3.81	1.24
1981	29,492	17,287	10,964	0.59	0.37	6.85	5.52	1.34
1982	31,710	19,213	11,172	0.61	0.35	6.18	4.93	1.25
1983	33,727	21,454	11,356	0.64	0.34	5.98	4.78	1.20
1984	36,186	23,965	11,395	0.66	0.31	5.87	4.67	1.20

1985	38,736	26,698	11,470	0.69	0.30	5.87	4.60	1.27
1986	40,726	28,964	11,335	0.71	0.28	5.35	4.14	1.22
1987	43,191	31,480	11,325	0.73	0.26	4.37	3.48	0.89
1988	46,492	33,922	11,757	0.73	0.25	4.09	3.04	1.05
1989	51,210	36,585	12,364	0.71	0.24	4.36	3.03	1.32
1990	56,108	37,999	13,455	0.68	0.24	5.94	4.45	1.49
1991	60,625	42,460	15,015	0.70	0.25	6.38	5.07	1.31
1992	62,981	44,163	16,584	0.70	0.26	5.09	4.23	0.86
1993	65,424	45,443	17,602	0.69	0.27	3.73	3.36	0.37
1994	67,656	46,186	18,097	0.68	0.27	2.47	2.18	0.29
1995	67,573	45,061	18,984	0.67	0.28	1.98	1.48	0.50
1996	67,696	44,026	19,952	0.65	0.29	0.96	0.73	0.23
1997	68,439	43,652	20,833	0.64	0.30	0.77	0.50	0.27
1998	68,996	43,563	21,460	0.63	0.31	0.72	0.36	0.36
1999	70,256	45,074	21,563	0.64	0.31	0.59	0.26	0.33
2000	72,094	47,347	21,521	0.66	0.30	0.47	0.21	0.26
2001	73,537	48,789	21,289	0.66	0.29	0.43	0.15	0.28
2002	74,420	50,506	21,096	0.68	0.28	0.35	0.08	0.27
2003	75,976	51,729	21,097	0.68	0.28	0.32	0.06	0.27
2004	77,609	53,262	20,922	0.69	0.27	0.31	0.05	0.26
2005	78,865	53,889	20,952	0.68	0.27	0.31	0.05	0.27
2006	80,139	54,798	21,592	0.68	0.27	0.39	0.11	0.28
2007	81,991	56,377	22,069	0.69	0.27	0.60	0.28	0.32
2008	83,232	55,913	23,260	0.67	0.28	0.75	0.32	0.43
2009	84,379	56,369	23,676	0.67	0.28	0.72	0.24	0.48

(*Continued*)

Table 1. (*Continued*)

Fiscal year	Balance of funds in banking at the fiscal year-end							
	Deposits (1)	Re-deposits to prefectural credit federations (2)	Loans (3)	Re-deposits/ deposits (4) = (2)/(1)	Loans/ deposits (5) = (3)/(1)	Average interest rate on re-deposits in prefectural credit federations (6)	Average interest rate on deposits in unit cooperatives (7)	Profit margin (8) = (7) − (6)
	billion yen					%		
2010	85,685	57,938	23,456	0.68	0.27	0.61	0.16	0.45
2011	88,064	60,259	23,213	0.68	0.26	0.56	0.11	0.45
2012	89,554	62,615	22,835	0.70	0.25	0.55	0.10	0.45
2013	91,370	64,664	22,645	0.71	0.25	0.56	0.09	0.47
2014	93,543	67,527	22,302	0.72	0.24	0.56	0.10	0.46
2015	95,761	70,206	21,983	0.73	0.23	0.56	0.10	0.46
2016	98,253	73,410	21,425	0.75	0.22	0.54	0.09	0.45
2017	1,01,131	76,408	21,499	0.76	0.21	0.53	0.07	0.45
2018	1,03,037	78,349	21,615	0.76	0.21	0.54	0.06	0.48
2019	1,03,931	78,711	21,865	0.76	0.21	0.52	0.05	0.47

Notes: 1. A fiscal year denotes the period between 1 April to 31 March.

2. Average interest rates are the ratio between the interest paid (or received) by unit cooperatives in the fiscal year and the outstanding amount at the end of the fiscal year.

Sources: MOF, Annual Economic Statistics; Norinchukin Research Institute, Fiscal Statistics of Agriculture, Forestry and Fisheries in Japan; MAFF, Statistics on Agricultural Cooperatives.

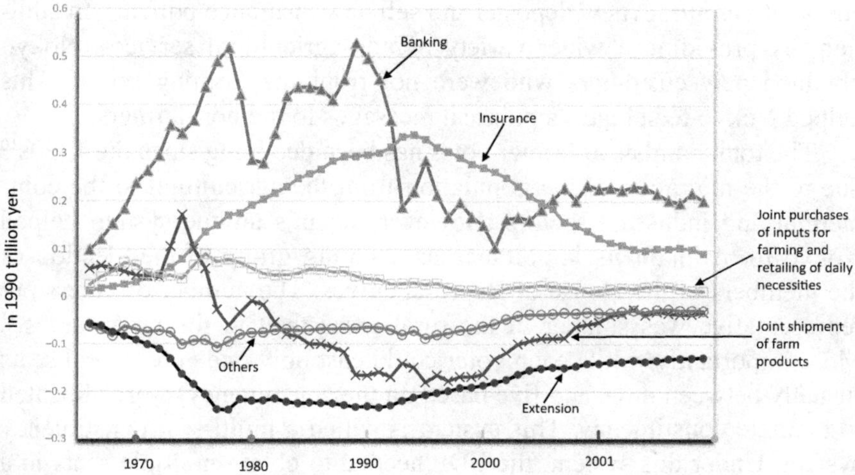

Figure 3. Profits of unit cooperatives' businesses.

Notes: 1. Profits are estimated by the author and deflated by a GDP deflator.
2. Profits from joint shipments include agricultural warehousing. Profit from joint purchase of inputs for farming and retailing of daily necessities cannot be estimated separately because of data limitations.

Sources: MAFF, Statistics on Agricultural Cooperatives; Cabinet Office, National Account of Japan.

week" when the employees visited the farmers to persuade them to deposit money into Nokyo.[9]

As shown in Figure 3, unit cooperatives became increasingly dependent on banking and insurance profits in the 1970s and 1980s. These two decades coincided with the period when the unit cooperatives expanded the scope of their activities under the slogan "Nokyo should promote not only agricultural production, but also overall community life in the rural areas." The unit cooperatives started various new businesses, including housing development companies and travel agencies, in the 1970s and 1980s. As Figure 3 shows, these new businesses were not particularly profitable; however, as the unit cooperatives were providing a wider range of services and offering greater convenience, they became more attractive to the local people (both farmers and non-farmers). This helped the unit

[9] Some of the unit cooperatives still have deposit promotion weeks as a ceremonial affair, although they are no longer profitable.

cooperatives attract new deposits and sell new insurance policies. In addition, by providing a wider variety of non-agricultural services, Nokyo obtained new customers who were not from the farming sector. This helped Nokyo to spread its political messages to the non-farmers.

The total number of farmer votes has been declining since the 1950s[10] due to the migration of the population from the agricultural to the commercial and industrial sectors. However, Japan's unique system helped Nokyo to maintain its importance as a voting group in the election of the members of the House of Representatives. The number of voters per representative was smaller in the rural areas than in the urban areas.[11] More importantly, while each voter could cast only one vote, plural seats (usually between three and five based on the constituency) were allocated to a single constituency. This system is called a multi-seat constituency system. Under this system, the LDP needed to obtain multiple seats in a constituency in order to have a majority in the House of Representatives. Since Nokyo was good at allocating farmers' votes among candidates from the LDP in each constituency, LDP needed to collaborate with Nokyo in elections.

Nokyo's Leadership in the Rice Autarky Policy Issue

Due to Japan's mountainous topography, the production costs of agricultural products in Japan are higher than that in other developed countries, such as Australia and the United States. For years, the Japanese government set (and still sets) various border protections against foreign agricultural products. For instance, Japan prohibited rice imports from any country when the trade negotiations at the Uruguay Round of the General Agreement on Tariffs and Trade (GATT) started in 1986. This rice autarky policy contradicted the GATT's rules. In addition, in the 1980s, Japan enjoyed a large trade surplus by exporting automobiles and machineries. Thus, it was inevitable for Japan to receive serious criticism on its rice autarky policy at the international negotiations.

---

[10] According to Japan's population census, the number of farm households hit a peak in 1950.

[11] See Mulgan (2000).

Japanese manufacturer groups, such as Keidanren (the Japanese abbreviation of the Japan Federation of Economic Organizations) and Doyukai (the Japanese abbreviation of the Japan Association of Corporate Executives), were active in advocating that Japan should open its rice market to foreign countries. As a counterargument against Keidanren and Doyukai, Nokyo asserted that rice was Japan's staple food and that it should be self-supplied in order to protect Japan from disruptions in its supply caused by international politics. In its appeal, Nokyo's logic, based on the "food security theory," succeeded in persuading the majority of Japanese families to support the rice autarky policy. According to a poll conducted by the Cabinet Office in 1988 to gauge public opinion, 71.2% of the respondents supported Japan's rice import prohibition.[12] Keidanren and Doyukai were also aware of the fact that if they demanded a complete liberalization of rice imports, the general public would turn against them. Therefore, they opted for the partial liberalization of rice imports by allowing for certain types of border protection (such as high tariff rates and import quotas) for rice imports.

In the final stages of the negotiations at the Uruguay Round of the GATT, it became difficult for Japan to participate in GATT without opening up its rice market to foreign countries. On 14 December 1993, Prime Minister Hosokawa announced that Japan would open its rice market by setting import quotas.[13] In retrospect, Hosokawa's decision was reasonable; however, his way of explaining it to the general public was less successful. As a result, Hosokawa aroused the ire of Japanese consumers and farmers.

Hosokawa was the first Prime Minister who did not belong to the LDP.[14] Although Hosokawa was not rich in experience at the House of Representative, his gentle presence in the mass media gave a good impression, and he was well received by the general public.[15] Assembling

---

[12] *Asahi Shinbun*, 22 February 1988, morning edition, p. 3.

[13] Hayami and Godo (1997) present details on the treatment of Japan's rice in the final agreements of the trade negotiations of the Uruguay Round of the GATT.

[14] Due to the Recruit Scandal, one of the biggest illicit political donation scandals in post-war Japan, the LDP was defeated in the election of members of the House of Representatives in July 1993. Accordingly, the LDP was removed from office for the first time since its establishment in 1955.

[15] Hosokawa was voted as the Prime Minister in his first term as a member of the House of Representatives.

the major leaders of eight political parties (excluding the LDP), the Hosokawa administration took office on 9 August 2013. At first, the new cabinet's approval rating (conducted by *Mainichi Newspapers*) was 75% — the highest in Japan's history. The future of the Hosokawa administration was riding on how long such a high approval rating would continue. Hosokawa's poor performance on rice import issue was fatal for his administration. The Hosokawa administration's approval rating kept declining after its announcement on rice imports. Finally, on 28 April 1994, Hosokawa resigned from the position of Prime Minister.[16]

Nokyo's Declining Economic and Political Power in the Middle of the 1990s

In retrospect, the early 1990s was the peak of Nokyo's economic and political influence. As can be seen in Figure 4, Nokyo's total number of officials kept on increasing until the early 1990s. Indeed, as described above, Nokyo was the leading decision-maker not only among farmers but also among the non-farmers in the negotiations at the Uruguay Round of the GATT.

However, Nokyo's economic and political power started to decline in the middle of 1990s. There were two major reasons for this decline: financial reforms and the reform of the electoral system.

Financial reform

Under the "armed convoys" policy, it was difficult for the foreign financial institutions to extend their businesses into the Japanese financial market. Thus, the North American and European governments repeatedly criticized the MOF. As a result, the MOF was compelled to abolish most of its "armed convoys" policy in the early 1990s. For example, the MOF removed the regulations on branch allocation, deposit interest rates, and insurance premiums. The MOF's financial deregulation negatively

[16] In addition to the rice import problem, there were two reasons behind Hosokawa's resignation from the position of Prime Minister: his failure in the introduction of new indirect taxes and suspicions regarding political donations.

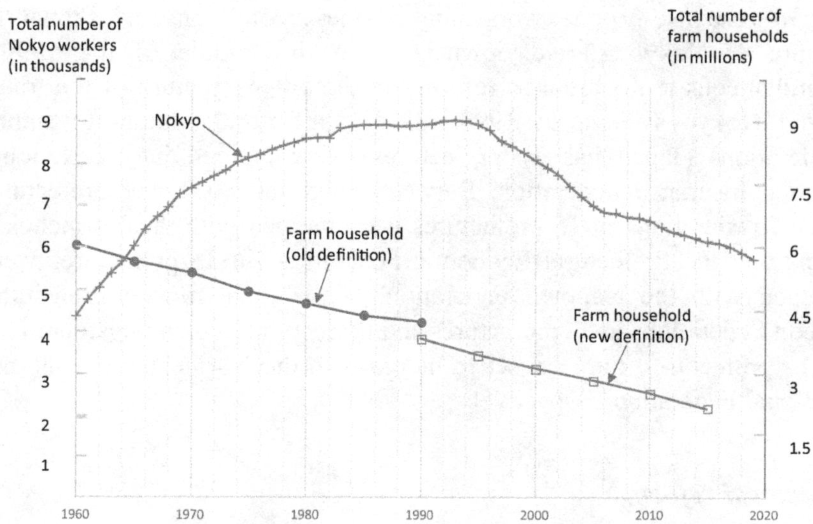

Figure 4. Total number of Nokyo workers relative to farm households.

Notes: For 1990–2015, a farm household is defined as a household that sells more than 15,000 yen of farm products in a year or holds more than 10 acres. For 1960–1990, a farm household is defined as a household that sells more than 15,000 yen of farm products in a year or holds more than 5 acres in the western part of Japan and 10 acres in the eastern part of Japan.

Sources: MAFF, Statistics on Agricultural Cooperatives, Agricultural Census.

impacted Nokyo. Figure 1 and column (8) of Table 1 show how the profitability of Nokyo's banking and insurance businesses declined in the middle of the 1990s; simultaneously, all businesses other than banking and insurance also remained unprofitable.

Further, in 1996, the Japanese financial market underwent the bitter ordeal of the *jusen* problem whereby housing loan companies, called *jusen*, went into default. While various banks lent money to the *jusen* companies, Nokyo was the largest lender. Thus, Nokyo's situation was critical. The MOF rescued Nokyo by injecting 685 billion yen into it. However, since Nokyo was the only financial institution rescued by the MOF, the mass media claimed that it so closely associated with the LDP. Such a claim invited resent from the general public. There were (and still are) various views about whether the amount of MOF's rescue deal was plausible and reasonable. The *jusen* problem reflected poorly on Nokyo, considering the general public's perspective.

In response to the worsening business conditions, as shown in Figure 4, Nokyo started downsizing in the middle of the 1990s. Simultaneously, it started to reform the three-tier structure of the traditional Nokyo system. In 1997, all 47 Prefectural Mutual Insurance Federations (Japan has 47 prefectures) were merged into a National Mutual Insurance Federation. Between 1998 and 2021, the Prefectural Credit Federations in 15 prefectures were merged with the Norinchukin Bank and the Prefectural Economic Federations in 35 prefectures were merged with the National Federation. While there remain Prefectural Credit Federations in 32 prefectures and Prefectural Economic Federations in 12 prefectures, they are set to merge with the Norinchukin Bank and National Federation, respectively.

Electoral reform

The Japanese political world was in turmoil in the early 1990s due to a scandal involving illicit political donations; it became known as the Recruit Scandal. It was said that the Recruit Scandal reflected a structural problem in Japanese politics, where plural candidates for the House of Representatives from the same political party in the same constituency tended to resort to pork-barrel spending because they were indifferent to political stances. In addition, the inequality in the value of a single vote started to increase urban citizens' discontent. Thus, lawmakers were under pressure to replace the electoral system for the House of Representatives.

In 1994, the bill for the entire revision of the electoral system for the House of Representatives was passed by the Diet. The former multi-seat constituency system was replaced by a single-seat system. This meant that Nokyo's strategy of allocating farmers' votes to plural candidates from the LDP in the same constituency collapsed. Following this revision, the inequality of the value of a single vote was reduced by reducing the number of seats for the constituencies of the rural areas and increasing the seats for the constituencies in the urban areas. This also reduced the value of farmers' (i.e., Nokyo members') votes. As a result, while Nokyo continued to support the LDP after the electoral reform, its influence on the LDP became weaker. Individual LDP lawmakers who had received Nokyo's support before the electoral reform may have remained sympathetic to Nokyo after the electoral reform; however, such feelings would fade over time.

Nokyo's Ordeal in the 2000s and 2010s

As mentioned above, for years, Nokyo had functioned as the *de facto* sub-government local office for the MAFF. However, due to the decline in the profitability of Nokyo's banking and financial activities, it could no longer afford to allocate time and personnel for collaborating with the MAFF in implementing agricultural programs. As a result, the MAFF terminated some of the programs; for example, the ACP was abolished in 2004. The global financial crisis in 2008 also negatively affected Nokyo. Among the Japanese financial institutions, Nokyo suffered the largest loss in securities investment in 2008. The total amount of Nokyo's hidden losses was estimated at approximately 1.9 trillion yen. Unlike the *jusen* case, the MOF did not provide any rescue money to Nokyo. As a result, Nokyo's banking business was at the point of collapsing. In order to stay in business, Nokyo collected 1.9 trillion yen from farmers in the form of an increase in Nokyo's capital. This experience increased farmers' dissatisfaction of Nokyo.

The Democratic Party (DP) was founded in 1998 and rode on an updraft in terms of political trends in voter preferences for change in the early 2010s, and it directed hostility toward Nokyo as the agricultural sector was an LDP stronghold. For the first 11 years since its establishment, the DP was an opposition party. Finally, it wrestled power from the LDP in September 2009 and remained in power until December 2012. During the 40 months during which the DP was in power, it cold-shouldered Nokyo, regarding it as a supporter of the LDP (i.e., an enemy of the DP). In addition, the DP administration repeatedly said that Nokyo was a part of the old guard that had prevented the agricultural industry from developing.

The LDP came back to power at the end of 2012 under the leadership of Shinzo Abe, who had headed the LDP from September 2011 to June 2020. Nokyo continued to receive cold treatment from the administration (this time from the LDP administration). This was because in the eyes of the general public, Abe wanted to present a dauntless attitude as a reformer against the old guard. In fact, Nokyo was already too weak to be called the old guard when the LDP came back to power. However, the image of a politically powerful Nokyo still persisted among the general public. Thus, Nokyo was a good object for Abe to showcase his dauntless attitude against the old guard. In 2015, by revising the Agricultural Cooperative Act, Abe removed the NCU from the Nokyo system.

While farmers are still allowed to participate in some political activities at Nokyo, it is no longer a key player in Japan's agricultural political arena.

Japan's aging population also had an impact on its farming sector in terms of the declining numbers of aging farmers and also shortage of manpower. Japan has to depend on importation of foreign workers (temporary or on various passes) to keep the sector going. Therefore, in Japan, an early impact of COVID-19 on the manpower situation arrived as early as February 2020 when a large number of Chinese workers returned home for reunions with their family during the Chinese Lunar New Year (LNY) season and could not come back to Japan (due to the Chinese authorities' complete lockdown policies) to harvest the products in vegetable farms in Japan.[17]

Conclusion

Nokyo used to be a strong opinion leader on Japan's agricultural issues. In particular, during the negotiations presented at the Uruguay Round of the GATT (1988–1994), representing most of the Japanese farmers, Nokyo took a firm stand against opening Japan's rice market to foreign countries. At that time, it did not yield to the Japanese manufacturers' groups, such as Keidanren and Doyukai, who stood for the liberalization of rice imports. In addition, Nokyo succeeded in persuading the majority of Japanese consumers to support its stance in the discussions on rice import liberalization issue. Nokyo's strong leadership on the issue was based on two advantages. First, Nokyo earned stable profits from its banking and insurance businesses. Second, Nokyo was good at canvassing farmers' votes.

However, the electoral and financial reforms in the middle of the 1990s deprived Nokyo of these advantages. As a result, Nokyo's economic and political power declined over the past 20 years. It is no longer a key player in agricultural political dynamics. It should be noted that earlier, Nokyo's close relationship with the LDP contradicted political

[17] Kobayashi, Yasuyuki (2020). "JA Zenchu with Japanese Farmers to Manage the COVID-19 Emergency" dated 2 July 2020 in World Farmers' Organisation [downloaded on 2 July 2020], available at https://www.wfo-oma.org/frmletter-2_2020/ja-zenchu-with-japanese-farmers-to-manage-the-covid-19-emergency/.

neutrality, which is essential in the ideology of corporatism. In that sense, it may be the time for Nokyo to return to pure corporatism.

References

Godo, Yoshihisa (2001). The Changing Economic Performance and Political Significance of Japan's Agricultural Cooperatives. Asia Pacific Economic Papers, No. 318.

Hayami, Yujiro and Yoshihisa Godo (1997). Economics and Politics of Rice Policy in Japan: A Perspective on the Uruguay Round. *Regionalism Versus Multilateral Trade Agreements*, eds. T. Ito and A. Krueger, Chicago, IL: University of Chicago Press, pp. 714–771.

Mulgan, Aurelia George (2000). *The Politics of Agriculture in Japan*, London and New York: Routledge.

Saeki, Naomi (1989). *Nogyo Keizaigaku Kogi: Lectures of Agricultural Economics*, Tokyo: University of Tokyo Press.

https://doi.org/10.1142/9789811253737_0003

Chapter 3

The End of the Agriculture Boom in Japan under the COVID-19 Pandemic

Yoshihisa Godo

Introduction

Starting in 2009, Japan witnessed a peculiar farming trend, with the domestic agricultural sector becoming the target of fulsome praise. Bookstores had entire sections devoted to books on upbeat topics such as "profitable farming" and "miraculous farming," and movies about farming were produced and screened in theaters. Television programs circulated various rosy stories on Japanese agriculture. Manufacturers showed an interest in starting new agriculture-related businesses such as food-processing and automation-style greenhouse farming. Successive prime ministers continued to nominate agriculture as one of the most promising industries in Japan. Japanese society was soaked in feverish imaginings of a prosperous and promising agricultural sector. This social phenomenon was called the "agriculture boom." However, due to the COVID-19 pandemic, the agriculture boom is now dying out. Why did the agriculture boom start? How did the COVID-19 pandemic affect the agriculture boom? By providing answers to these questions, this chapter aims to describe the changing political dynamics of Japanese agriculture.

Agricultural Disputes during the GATT Uruguay Round

Social phenomena in Japan are often associated with the performance of the manufacturing sector, which is the largest contributor to the gross domestic product (GDP) of the country.[1] Opinions from manufacturers' groups, such as Keidanren (the Japanese abbreviation of the Japan Federation of Economic Organizations) and Doyukai (the Japanese abbreviation of the Japan Association of Corporate Executives), are critical of the Japanese government's policymaking. As discussed in detail below, the problems of the agricultural sector are not exceptional. Thus, before discussing the agriculture boom, it is useful to review how manufacturers have historically viewed Japanese agriculture.

From the 1950s to the early 1990s, Japan's GDP grew faster than any other major developed country.[2] The manufacturing sector spearheaded this high-speed growth.[3] Based on its strong competitive power in the international market, Japan was aggressively exporting manufactured commodities. Japan's exports of manufactured commodities, labeled "concentrated exports," frustrated European and North American governments, which consequently suffered mass closures of factories and faced high unemployment.

---

[1] According to estimates of the Cabinet Office, the manufacturing sector contributed 23.5% to Japan's GDP in 2019. As of December 2020, 10.5 billion people are employed in the manufacturing sector, which accounts for 15.8% of Japan's total employment. These data are available from the homepage of the Cabinet Office: http://www.stat.go.jp/data/roudou/sokuhou/tsuki/pdf/gaiyou.pdf and https://www.esri.cao.go.jp/jp/sna/data/data_list/kakuhou/files/2019/2019_kaku_top.html.

[2] According to Angus Maddison's historical database (http://www.ggdc.net/maddison/oriindex.htm, last updated in March 2010), the average growth rate in Japan (in 1990 International Geary-Khamis dollars) between 1950 and 1990 was 6.90% per annum while that in West Europe and the Western Offshoots was 3.73% and 3.57%, respectively.

[3] The Cabinet Office provides their estimates on GDP by economic sector for 1970 and thereafter (https://www.esri.cao.go.jp/jp/sna/data/data_list/kakuhou/files/files_kakuhou.html). According to them, the share of the manufacturing sector in GDP increased from 26.3% to 28.2% between 1970 and 1990. Considering that there was a mass labor movement from the agricultural sector to the manufacturing sector in the 1950s and 1960s (see Hayami (1988)), it is safe to say that the share of the manufacturing sector in Japan's GDP continued to increase from 1950 to 1990.

However, the international competitive power of the Japanese agricultural sector was (and still is) weak because the Japanese topography is too mountainous to utilize high-technology agricultural machinery. However, Japanese farmers could (and still can) survive because the government established (and continues to implement) border protections such as import quotas and tariffs on agricultural imports. For instance, when Japan's rice price was more than twice the international level,[4] the Japanese government prohibited rice imports until 1994 (except for emergency rice imports and Thai rice, which is the main ingredient of Awamori, Okinawa's local liquor).

Before the World Trade Organization (WTO) was established in 1995, the General Agreement on Tariffs and Trade (GATT) provided the regulatory framework of international trade. The GATT required member countries to promote free competition in the international market. Thus, Japan's import barriers for agricultural commodities naturally received serious criticism in international trade negotiations and talks. This criticism reached a critical level in the GATT Uruguay Round trade negotiations (1986–94). Japan's import prohibition on rice was so severely criticized that it became difficult for the Japanese government to stay in the GATT without opening its rice market to foreign countries.

Keidanren and Doyukai were active in presenting their opinion that the Japanese government should reduce (or remove) the import barriers for agricultural commodities.[5] In so doing, they repeatedly referred to the "international division of labor theory," which is a popular concept in economics.[6] The international division of labor theory claims that each country's GDP is maximized if the country concentrates on producing its internationally competitive commodities under a free international market system. In the years of the GATT Uruguay Round trade negotiations, Japan's manufactured commodities were internationally competitive while Japan's agricultural commodities were internationally uncompetitive. Thus, the international division of labor theory was a strong supporter for the Japanese manufacturers but an adversary for the Japanese farmers.

---

[4] Godo and Owens (1988) provide detailed information on the border price difference of rice.

[5] For examples, see Japan Federation of Economic Organizations (1990).

[6] For examples, see Moroi (1990). Moroi was the former Vice Chairperson of the Japan Association of Corporate Executives.

As a counterargument against Keidanren and Doyukai, Zenchu (the Japanese abbreviation of the Central Union of Agricultural Cooperatives) asserted that agricultural commodities were daily necessities whose social value is much higher than could be captured by market prices, and that the international division of labor theory should not be applied to agricultural commodities.[7] Zenchu argued that to protect Japan from distractions in international politics, it should not increase agricultural imports. This logic, called the "food security theory," appealed emotionally (and continues to appeal) to the Japanese. There was (and still is) a tendency among the Japanese to maintain a nostalgic image of agriculture and to be tolerant of their government's protection for the sector (including agricultural subsidies).[8] According to a public-opinion poll conducted by the Cabinet Office in 1988, 71.2% of respondents supported Japan's rice import prohibition.[9]

Keidanren and Doyukai were also aware that, if they demanded a complete removal of agricultural protection from the government, the general public would resent them. Thus, they requested for a partial reduction (not entire removal) of the agricultural protection. However, essentially, they advocated for the international division of labor theory.[10]

By the end of the GATT Uruguay Round trade negotiations, the Japanese government finally agreed to open its rice market by setting import quotas.[11]

---

[7] Japan has a unique system of agricultural cooperatives, which is commonly called Nokyo. The Nokyo system has a three-tier structure. Unit cooperatives in the villages, towns, and cities make up the first level. The Prefectural Central Unions of Agricultural Cooperatives in the prefectures make up the second level. Each prefecture has its own Prefectural Central Union, to which all the unit cooperatives in the prefecture belong. At the third and top level, the National Central Union of Agricultural Cooperatives supervises all the unit cooperatives in Japan through Prefectural Central Unions. Unit cooperatives are in direct contact with farmers. Each unit cooperative has its own jurisdiction, and their jurisdictions should not overlap. An overwhelming majority of Japanese farmers join their local unit cooperatives but are not under any legal obligation to do so. The Nokyo system has often functioned as a *de facto* sub-governmental body. For more details of the Nokyo system, see Godo (2001), (2007), (2014), and (2015).

[8] Francks (2006) compares the scene of farming to a powerful weapon in the armory of the Japanese advertising industry.

[9] See Cabinet Office (1988).

[10] See Japan Federation of Economic Organizations (1990).

[11] Details of the results on the GATT Uruguay Round agreements on Japan's rice imports are discussed by Hayami and Godo (1997).

The Idea of "Aggressive Agriculture" in the Lost Two Decades

The middle of the 1990s was a drastic turning point for the Japanese economy. Until then, Japan had been appraised as the most successful country among developed countries. "Japan as Number One" was one of the most popular phrases in the international arena throughout the 1980s.[12] Thereafter, however, Japan has been declaimed as the most unsuccessful.[13] Japan's average annual growth rate of nominal GDP between 1995 and 2019 was only 0.31%.[14] This prolonged recession is termed the "Lost Two Decades."[15]

During the "Lost Two Decades," newly industrialized countries such as China deprived Japan of its market share in the international market for manufactured commodities. Moreover, some of Japan's top manufacturers, such as NEC and Nissan, recorded huge losses and reduced their operations. It became clear that Japan had lost the advantage in the production of manufactured commodities.

Reflecting Japanese manufacturers' weakening international competitive power, after the GATT Uruguay Round trade negotiations, Keidanren and Doyukai changed their opinions. They ceased to refer to the international division of labor theory. Instead, Keidanren and Doyukai became concerned with the withdrawal of government protection for Japanese manufacturers. Simultaneously, however, Keidanren and Doyukai did not want to publicly declare that the Japanese manufacturing sector was trailing behind in the international market for manufactured commodities (such a declaration would have been too disgraceful for Keidanren and Doyukai).

---

[12] "Japan as the Number One," appeared as the title of Vogel's (1979) book. This book was an international best seller.

[13] According to Angus Maddison's historical database (see note 1), the annual growth rate in Japan (in 1990 International Geary-Khamis dollars) between 1990 and 2008 was 1.25% while that in West Europe and in the Western Offshoots was 2.05% and 2.79%, respectively.

[14] According to the Cabinet Office's estimates (see note 1), nominal GDP in 1995 and 2019 are 521.6 and 561.3 trillion yen, respectively.

[15] Caballero *et al.* (2008) provide a comprehensive analysis on the major causes of the "Lost Two Decades."

In 2004, Japan Economic Research Institute, a private research institute founded and sponsored by major manufacturers' groups including Keidanren and Doyukai, submitted a new idea for the revitalization of Japanese agriculture, called "aggressive agriculture."[16] The idea of "aggressive agriculture" can be summarized as:

(1) Japanese agriculture has high potential.
(2) Current farmers are too old-fashioned to realize that potential.
(3) If non-agricultural companies start farming, they will introduce modern technology and management.
(4) By combining agriculture and other businesses (e.g., green tourism, food processing, and restaurants), the Japanese agricultural sector will be more profitable. This combination, called "the sixth industrialization" should be the key strategy for revitalizing the agricultural industry.[17]
(5) Non-agricultural companies could advocate and promote the sixth industrialization.
(6) The Japanese government should provide financial and institutional support for non-agricultural companies' entry into agriculture and for their involvement in the sixth industrialization process.

Keidanren and Doyukai are aware that the Japanese are tolerant toward their government regarding the allocation of subsidies and border protection for the agricultural sector. By advocating aggressive agriculture, Keidanren and Doyukai used agriculture (including

[16] Japan Economic Research Institute (2004) presented the theoretical framework for aggressive agriculture.

[17] In economics textbooks, it is common to classify production activities into three categories: the primary industry (the industry that is concerned with obtaining or providing natural raw materials for conversion into commodities and products for the consumer); the secondary industry (the industry that converts the raw materials provided by primary industry into commodities and products for the consumer); and the tertiary industry (the part of a country's economy concerned with the provision of services). The idea of the sixth industrialization is that by combining agricultural products (commodities of the primary industry) with manufacturing such as food processing (the secondary industry) and services such as tourism (the tertiary industry), agriculture would be more profitable. This mechanism is compared to the mathematical equation: primary (1) + secondary (2) + tertiary (3) = sixth (6). This is the origin of the name, sixth industrialization.

agriculture-related businesses) as a tool for campaigning for the withdrawal of support (including subsidies) from the government.

When aggressive agriculture was announced, it did not elicit much attention from the Japanese general public. However, as discussed in the next section, after the 2008 global financial crisis, "aggressive agriculture" was included in the agriculture boom.

The Beginning of the Agriculture Boom after the 2008 Global Financial Crisis

The collapse of Lehman Brothers in the United States triggered the 2008 global financial crisis; however, among the major advanced countries, the crisis inflicted the heaviest damage on Japan.[18] Japan's nominal GDP shrank by more than 8% from 2007 to 2009.[19] In contrast, the Chinese economy kept growing. As a result, China's GDP surpassed that of Japan.[20] This hurt Japanese national pride and sentiments. Furthermore, anti-China sentiment in Japan, became more acrimonious after the massive riots in major Chinese cities in 2005 against the Japanese prime minister's worshipping at the Yasukuni Shrine. The view that China's high-speed economic growth deprived Japan of its erstwhile economic power became popular among the Japanese. Simultaneously, the Japanese became eager to hear platitudes and optimistic stories (whether real or fake) that "Japan is still Number One in the world (particularly against China)" in some sectors. In this respect, the agricultural sector lent itself to the creation of such stories. Unlike manufactured commodities, the quality of agricultural commodities is difficult to measure; this makes it easier to create a story claiming that "Japan is still Number One" (in reality, however, the quality of agricultural commodities in other Asian countries, including China, is improving). In addition, the food poison scandals in China, such as the melamine-laced powdered milk, was greatly reported and sensationalized in Japan. Thus, the Japanese general

---

[18] For example, see "Keiki Kaifuku Nihon Kigyo Kaigaizeini Okure (Japanese Companies lag behind Foreign Companies)" *Nikkei Newspaper* (morning edition), 3 June 2010.

[19] According to the Cabinet Office's estimates (see note 1), nominal GDP in 2007 and 2009 were 593.3 and 494.9 trillion yen, respectively.

[20] Chinese GDP surpassed Japanese GDP in 2010. However, this was already expected in 2009.

public indulged in a feeling of superiority over China with regard to agriculture.

Therefore, the agriculture boom occurred after the 2008 global financial crisis. Reflecting the Japanese general public's increasing expectations from agriculture, politicians started circulating rosy stories (colored by the imagination) on agriculture. The *cholas* of "Japanese agriculture is the growing industry" developed among the Japanese general public and politicians. Public imagination was captivated by fictional stories of farming. In every notable bookstore, special corners had been dedicated to showcase the romantic aspects of farming and agricultural success stories. On TV, "pundits" proudly offered explanations on the "unrivaled level of Japanese farming technology." Various slogans related to farming were successively coined, such as "local production for local consumption," "agro-commerce-industry collaboration," "semi-agricultural, semi-this and that," and the "sixth industrialization." Corporate farming ventures and the younger generation's engagement in agriculture were being widely promoted. Mired in a protracted economic slump described as the "Lost Two Decades," farming had become one of those few areas that provided the public with positive news (while many of them were fabricated stories).

The agriculture boom coincided with manufacturers groups' ideas on aggressive agriculture. The government designed the agricultural policy reflecting the idea of aggressive agriculture and prepared new subsidies for the sixth industrialization and non-agricultural companies' entry to farming. Additionally, it amended the Agricultural Land Act to promote non-agricultural companies' involvement in agriculture.

As an indicator of the flux and reflux of the agriculture boom, this chapter uses the number of newspaper articles that contain "agriculture" and "growing industry" as keywords, as can be seen Figure 1. This figure shows that the agriculture boom started in 2009 and ended in 2020. During these 12 years, the prime minister of Japan changed five times: Taro Aso of the Liberal Democratic Party to (from September 2008 to September 2009) Yukio Hatoyama of the Democratic Party (from September 2009 to June 2010), Naoto Kan of the Democratic Party (from June 2010 to September 2011), Noda of the Democratic Party (from September 2011 to December 2012), Abe of the Liberal Democratic Party (from December 2012 to September 2020), and Yoshihide Suga of the Liberal Democratic Party (from September 2020 to the present). Except for Suga, the other prime ministers had declared agriculture to be the most

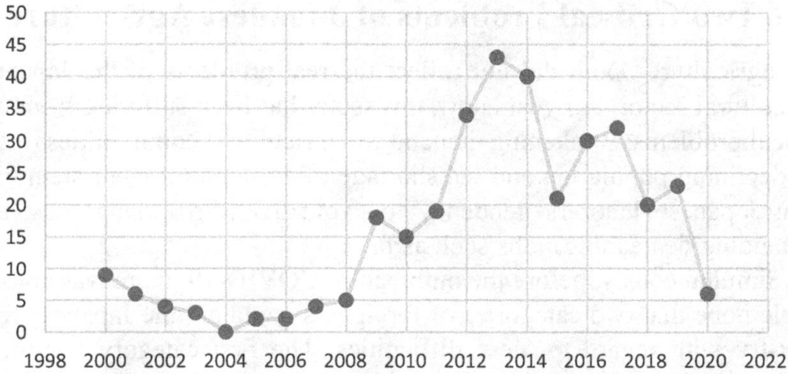

Figure 1. The number of articles containing "agriculture" and "growing industry" as keywords.

Source: Kikuzo II Visual (online article database provided by Asahi Shimbun Company).

promising industry. It should be noted that Abe had also been the prime minister from September 2006 to September 2007. During those 13 months, Abe had never nominated agriculture as Japan's growing industry. After Abe stepped down from office, Japanese agriculture received two serious shocks: the outbreak of foot-mouth disease in 2010 and the radioactivity pollution problem in 2011, which was caused by the accident at the Fukushima Daiichi Nuclear Power Station.[21] Ignoring these two major incidents, as soon as Abe returned to power in December 2012, he started projecting agriculture as Japan's most promising industry. This proves that the agriculture boom did not stem from objective evidence on the Japanese agricultural sector. In fact, the two critical problems of Japanese agriculture had been out of focus during the agriculture boom.

---

[21] For years, Japan maintained a disease-free status with regard to foot-mouth disease. However, in March 2010, an outbreak of foot-and-mouth disease was reported in Miyazaki Prefecture, one of Japan's largest livestock concentrations. By killing 298 heads of cows and pigs in four months aimed at preventing further infection, the Miyazaki prefectural government succeeded in eradicating foot-and-mouth disease. However, many bulls with high-quality seed were killed. The Miyazaki prefectural government estimated that the total loss due to foot-and-mouth disease was 235 billion yen. While the International Epizootic Office approved Japan's return to a disease-free status from foot-mouth disease in February 2012, some countries continued prohibiting beef imports from Japan (for example, beef imports from Japan have been prohibited in China since April 2010).

The Two Critical Problems of Japanese Agriculture

The agriculture boom did not reflect the real problems of the Japanese agricultural sector. For years now, this sector has been suffering from two critical problems: weakening demand for agricultural commodities due to the declining population and the shortage of agricultural labor stemming from Japanese laborers' tendency to avoid 3D (dirty, dangerous, and demanding/demeaning) jobs such as farming.

Simultaneously, before the outbreak of COVID-19, there was considerable hope that two categories of foreigners could aid the Japanese food industry with regard to these difficulties. The first category comprises foreign tourists who exhibit a strong demand for Japanese food. As seen in Table 1, foreign tourist numbers rose rapidly.[22] According to a Japan

Table 1. Foreign tourists entering Japan.

Year	Visitor arrivals (in thousands)	Change (%)	Year	Visitor arrivals (in thousands)	Change (%)
1990	3,236	14.1	2005	6,728	9.6
1991	3,533	9.2	2006	7,334	9.0
1992	3,582	1.4	2007	8,347	13.8
1993	3,410	−4.8	2008	8,351	0.0
1994	3,468	1.7	2009	6,790	−18.7
1995	3,345	−3.5	2010	8,611	26.8
1996	3,837	14.7	2011	6,219	−27.8
1997	4,218	9.9	2012	8,358	34.4
1998	4,106	−2.7	2013	10,364	24.0
1999	4,438	8.1	2014	13,413	29.4
2000	4,757	7.2	2015	19,737	47.1
2001	4,772	0.3	2016	24,040	21.8
2002	5,239	9.8	2017	28,691	19.3
2003	5,212	−0.5	2018	31,192	8.7
2004	6,138	17.8	2019	31,882	2.2

Source: Ministry of Justice.

[22] As seen in Table 1, Japan witnessed a two-digit-percent decrease from the previous year in the total number of foreign visitors in 2009 and 2011. The first one is attributable to the global recession caused by the 2008 global financial crisis and the second one to the radiation accident at the Fukushima Nuclear Power Plant. In addition, Table 1 shows slowdown

Travel Online Community survey, "enjoying Japanese foods" is the strongest motivation to visit Japan for many foreign tourists.[23]

Indeed, foreign tourists/visitors seemed heavily inclined toward luxury agricultural commodities, such as Kobe beef, Awayuki white strawberry, and Satoh Nishiki cherries, which were (and remain) unaffordable for most Japanese consumers. Chinese tourists are so generous with their money while purchasing highly priced agricultural commodities that their aggressive shopping style is called *Bakugai* (its literal translation is "explosive shopping spree").

Second, foreign manual laborers were expected to increase in numbers because the government implemented new schemes which allow the entry of foreign manual laborers. In recent years, the Japanese government has held the principle that unskilled foreign laborers (including manual laborers) should not be allowed to work in Japan. This principle reflects Japanese citizens' anxiety that foreign laborers may deprive local workers of job opportunities and disturb the community's social order. Nonetheless, Japan continued to accept unskilled foreign laborers.[24] For example, the government allows foreigners to perform manual labor under the visa status of "Technical Intern Trainees" under certain stipulated conditions. In principle, the workplace of each technical intern trainee is determined before his or her entry to Japan.

Previously, the maximum length of stay for technical intern trainees was 3 years. However, in 2017, it was extended to 5 years. In addition, in 2018, the Japanese government launched a new visa status called "Specified Skilled Worker" for *de facto* unskilled foreign laborers.[25] The Japanese government nominated 14 industrial fields, including agriculture, for specified skilled workers. Foreigners could obtain the visa status of a specified skilled worker in two ways. The first is an

---

of the rate of increase in the total number of foreign visitors in 2018 and 2019. This is attributable to the decrease of Korean visitors under the anti-Japan campaign.

[23] Details of the survey are available at https://action.jnto.go.jp/library/1159. Japan Travel Online Community is the Japanese government's agent for supporting tourism in Japan.

[24] This chapter only provides an outline of the system for accepting *de facto* foreign laborers. For further details, see Godo and Lim (2017).

[25] There are two visa types for specified skilled workers: Type I and Type II. Since Type II is applicable only for construction and shipbuilding, this chapter only discusses Type I. More details on the visa status of specified skilled workers are provided in Godo (2019).

automatic transition from the technical intern training on completion of the training period. The other is to take an examination whereby foreigners are tested on their Japanese language proficiency and working skills. Specified skilled workers are allowed to stay in Japan for up to 5 years. Moreover, specified skilled workers have the freedom to change their place of work (as far as the workplaces are in the designated industrial fields).

COVID-19 in Japan

The first case of COVID-19 in Japan was detected on 15 January 2020. A person who had stayed in Wuhan from 3 January to 6 January showed symptoms of COVID-19. On 27 January 2020, the government designated COVID-19 as a "Designated Infectious Disease" and patients were forced into quarantine. On 1 February 2020, the Japanese government prohibited people who had been in Wuhan in the last two weeks from entering Japan. Since then, the immigration prohibition gradually extended to other regions and countries. The number of countries from which Japan prohibited immigration reached 129 on 3 July 2020, that is, Japan refused entrance to people from most countries in the world. The 2020 Tokyo Olympic Games were also postponed until 2021.

The spread of COVID-19 in Japan was slower than in Europe and North America. For example, as of 3 June 2020, Japan's death rate for COVID-19 was 7 persons per million. Nonetheless, the spread of COVID-19 disturbed Japanese society. The government presented guidelines on business hours for shops and restaurants and restricted the number of people gathering at theaters, restaurants, and stadiums. These restraints have hindered economic activities. Thus, the government has launched various economic programs to mitigate the economic damage. On 7 April 2020, the government announced its emergency compensation plan for medium- and small-size enterprises, whereby those who suffered a significant loss as a result of the COVID-19 pandemic may receive up to 2 million yen. On 16 April 2020, the government decided to provide emergent subsidy of 100,000 yen to each family. In August 2020, it launched a large subsidy program for promoting severely affected businesses such as food services and tourism. However, these programs were suspended when the number of COVID-19 patients started increasing from 28 December 2020.

The End of the Agriculture Boom

Figure 1 shows that the agricultural boom ended in 2020. Indeed, since Yoshihide Suga became the Prime Minister in July 2020, he has not declared agriculture to be a promising industry.

From 2008 to 2019, the average annual growth rate of agricultural GDP was 0.14% while that of total GDP was 0.56%. This means that the agricultural sector restrained Japan's economic growth even during the period of the agriculture boom. Thus, the agriculture boom can be viewed as an illusion. Thus, it was inevitable that the agriculture boom would end soon. The remaining question is, why was it 2020? A precise answer would entail a detailed investigation and more time. However, for the moment, it is possible to present the following two points as working hypotheses.

First, the inflow of foreigners was blocked in 2020 because of the COVID-19 pandemic. As a result, the two critical problems in the Japanese agricultural sector, the declining demand for agricultural products and the shortage of agricultural laborers, became serious and the mass media began to reporting repeatedly on the realities of Japanese agriculture in the midst of the COVID-19 pandemic. This prevented the public from enjoying illusive stories on Japanese agriculture.

Second, the COVID-19 pandemic caused Keidanren and Doyukai to ardently request the government to support manufacturers' main businesses (not new businesses related to agriculture). Previously, they hesitated at making such requests since they do not like acknowledging that Asian countries (China in particular), were better at manufacturing than Japan. In theory, if Japanese manufacturers were defeated by free competition, they should accept the responsibility instead of shifting the responsibility onto the government. For this reason, these bodies used agriculture, in the name of "aggressive agriculture," as a tool for advocating the withdrawal of government support. However, the COVID-19 pandemic is the natural disaster, for which the manufacturers are not responsible. Thus, Keidanren and Doyukai have been emboldened to ask for financial support from the government. In that sense, the relevance of agriculture for manufacturers has ended.

Conclusion

The agriculture boom, which started in 2009, can be viewed as one of the after-effects of the 2008 global financial crisis. Using Japanese agriculture as a tool to create rosy (but empty) stories, the Japanese general public, who faced a loss of national pride in no longer being the second largest economy in the world and the leader in Asia, tried to forget the bitter reality of China's rising economic superiority to Japan. Japanese manufacturers who were affected due to the crisis and lost competitive power in the international market for manufactured commodities, tried to draw on the government's support by starting new businesses related to farming. While expectations for Japanese agriculture surged among the general public and manufacturers, it did not stem from reality. Finally, by restricting the inflow of foreigners, the COVID-19 pandemic exposed Japanese agriculture's vulnerability, that it may be unable to survive without foreign tourists' strong demands for food and foreign manual laborers' inputs into the farms and their operations. In addition, Japanese manufacturers re-dedicated themselves to keeping their main businesses afloat and successful (instead of starting new businesses related to farming) during the economic turmoil of the COVID-19 pandemic. As such, the agriculture boom is now dying out.

While a vaccine for the COVID-19 virus is anticipated, even after its eradication, strict quarantines will remain the norm and a long-term effects of COVID-19 will remain. There is a theory that environmental destruction, which has globally accelerated through human economic activities, will increase the possibilities of new viruses emerging.[26] The COVID-19 pandemic has increased the credibility of this theory. Now, international society has become more cautious about the liberalization of cross-border movement of labor and tourists, because these movements increase the risk of new infectious diseases. Previously, the Japanese agricultural sector expected foreign tourists' strong demand for Japanese foods to bolster the industry. Additionally, a significant inflow of foreign workers could relieve the labor shortages at workplaces such as farms. However, the Japanese agricultural sector will now need to find alternative solutions.

References

Caballero, Ricardo J., Takeo Hoshi, and Anil K. Kashyap (2008). Zombie Lending and Depressed Restructuring in Japan. *American Economic Review*, 98(5), 1943–1977.

[26] For examples, see Paolo (2020).

Cabinet Office (1988). *Nihon-jin no Shokuseikatsu to Shokuryo* (Eating Habits and Food Problems in Japan).

Francks, Penelope (2006). *Rural Economic Development in Japan*, Routledge.

Godo, Yoshihisa (2001). "The Changing Economic Performance and Political Significance of Japan's Agricultural Cooperatives," *Pacific Economic Papers* (Australia-Japan Research Centre, Australian National University), No. 318.

Godo, Yoshihisa (2007). "The Puzzle of Small Farming in Japan," *Pacific Economic Papers* (Australia–Japan Research Centre, Australian National University), No. 365.

Godo, Yoshihisa (2014). "The Significance of Non-farmers in Japanese Agricultural Cooperatives," *FFTC Agricultural Policy Database* (Food & Fertilizer Technology Center for the Asian and Pacific Region), 4 July 2014, available at https://ap.fftc.org.tw/article/699.

Godo, Yoshihisa (2015). "Estimating Agricultural Cooperatives' Share in Agricultural Input and Output Markets," *FFTC Agricultural Policy Database* (Food & Fertilizer Technology Center for the Asian and Pacific Region), 2 March, available at https://ap.fftc.org.tw/article/821.

Godo, Yoshihisa (2019). "Japan's New policy on Foreign Laborers and its Impact on the Agricultural Industry," FFTC Agricultural Policy Database (Food & Fertilizer Technology Center for the Asian and Pacific Region), 22 November, available at https://ap.fftc.org.tw/article/1633.

Godo, Yoshihisa and Lincoln Owens (1998). "An Estimation of the Border Price Ratio of Rice in Japan," *The Papers and Proceedings of Economics* (Meiji Gakuin University), No. 605, January.

Godo, Yoshihisa, and Tai Wei Lim (2017). "Trainee Schemes in Japan," *EAI Background Brief* (National University of Singapore) No. 1232.

Hayami, Yujiro (1988). *Japanese Agriculture Under Siege*, Palgrave Macmillan.

Hayami, Yujiro, and Yoshihisa Godo (1997). Economics and Politics of Rice Policy in Japan: A Perspective on the Uruguay Round. *Regionalism versus Multilateral Trade Agreements*, eds. Takatoshi Ito and Anne O. Krueger, University of Chicago Press.

Japan Economic Research Institute (2004). *Nosei no Bappon Kaikaku* (The Fundamental Reform on Japan's Agricultural Policy).

Japan Federation of Economic Organizations (1988). *Shokuhin Kogyomuke Kokunai Nousanbutsu no Ohabana Kosuto Sakugenwo Motomaru Teigen* (A Proposal for Cost Reduction of Domestic Agricultural Products for Food Processing).

Japan Federation of Economic Organizations (1990). *Uruguai Raundo no Seiko wo Nozomu* (The Uruguay Round Trade Negotiations Should be Successful).

Moroi, Ken (1990). "Nogyo Hogo Shokkan wa Jidai Okure" (Japan's Agricultural Protection and the Rice Control System are outdated), *Nikkei Business Daily*, morning edition, 23 July.

Paolo, Giordano (2020). *How Contagion Works: Science, Awareness and Community in Times of Global Crises — The Short Essay that Helped Change the COVID-19 Debate*, Weidenfeld & Nicolson.

Vogel, Ezra F. (1979). *Japan as Number One: Lessons for America*, Harvard University Press.

Part 2

COVID-19 and the Community

https://doi.org/10.1142/9789811253737_0004

Chapter 4

COVID-19 and Overseas Chinese Community in Japan: A Case Study of Yokohama Chinatown

Elim Wong and Wilson Lee

Introduction: COVID-19 and Japan

The year of 2020 was extremely difficult for everyone around the world. The whole world was caught by surprise when it was struck by the COVID-19 coronavirus pandemic starting from 23 January 2020 when it was publicly revealed by the Chinese authorities. According to World Health Organization (WHO), the outbreak of COVID-19 pandemic started with "a media statement by the Wuhan Municipal Health Commission from their website on cases of "viral pneumonia" in Wuhan, People's Republic of China."[1] China's neighbor Japan reported the first confirmed case on 16 January 2020. The date marked the beginning of the tough economic time in Yokohama Chinatown because the COVID-19 patient zero is an ethnic Chinese living in Kanagawa prefecture, where the 160-year-old Chinatown is located. The Japanese mass media reporting has had a great impact on the Chinatown business, since the Japanese people started to avoid visiting the Chinatown, where large

[1] "WHO's COVID-19 response," World Health Organization, accessed 3 August 2021, available at https://www.who.int/emergencies/diseases/novel-coronavirus-2019/interactive-timeline#!.

number of Chinese people can be found, in order to minimize the chances of getting infected. On social media, some Japanese netizens encouraged the public to "stay away from the Chinese" and not to visit Yokohama Chinatown. Yokohama Chinatown has turned into a ghost town from a reputable sightseeing spot among domestic tourists, with its 500 restaurants and shops shut since January 2020.

Kanagawa prefecture, being part of the Tokyo metropolitan region, is located south of Tokyo, the capital city of Japan. The prefecture hosts the third largest population in Japan. Given its historical background, Yokohama is one of the most well-known cities in Kanagawa prefecture. When Japan was forced to open up to the West with the Convention of Kanagawa in 1854, the favorable location of Yokohama turned the city into the residential area for the Western traders and officials. Many of the Western traders hired Chinese men from Guangdong area of China to Japan as translators and workers. These Chinese men were not allowed to live in the same residential area as the Westerners. In fact, they were banned from living outside a certain space, which marked the beginning of the establishment of Yokohama Chinatown in the mid-1850s. After 160 years have passed, this Chinatown is still the largest Chinatown in Japan, second largest in the world, and one of the most-visited sightseeing spots in Japan that attracts more than 16 million visitors per year.

During the pandemic period, the Kanagawa prefecture became a highly searched keyword on social media search engine because of its five "FIRSTs": the "first" confirmed COVID-19 case in Japan reported on 16 January 2020, the "first" widespread incident of Diamond Princess cruise that landed at the port of Yokohama on 3 February 2020, the "first" death in Japan occurred in Kanagawa prefecture on 13 February 2020, the "first" death from the new UK coronavirus variant on 16 March 2021 and the "first" death from the new India coronavirus variant on 31 May 2021. The five "FIRSTs" has a great impact on Yokohama Chinatown because they scared the tourists away from visiting the Chinatown. Many of the restaurants and shops have to close temporarily in order to save operational costs. Out of the many shops and restaurants in Kanagawa prefecture, however, a number of them began to put the blame on ethnic Chinese people. According to *Asahi Shimbun*, a Japanese snack shop in Hakone posted a notice on the entrance, titled "Chinese people is prohibited to enter the shop" and the textual narrative of the notice was that "Chinese people can spread coronavirus and should be banned from entering the shop. Please do not come to Hakone and Japan. But please do not confuse Hong Kong people and Taiwanese with Chinese people."[2] The notice provoked and received a lot of responses on the Internet. Although a number of people supported the ban on Chinese people from restaurants and shops, more people became concerned about the spread of criticisms and discrimination toward ethnic Chinese people, worsening the relationship between Japanese and Chinese peoples and societies.

Similar critical messages directed toward Chinese tourists have also flooded social media outlet Twitter after the appearance of the notice at Hakone. *Nishi Nippon News* reported how netizens responded to tourists from China who arrived in Fukuoka after the outbreak of COVID-19 in Japan. On 29 January 2020, a tweet on Twitter titled "(sad new) Notice of the end of Fukuoka #please forward" mentioned the arrival of a cruise from China at Fukuoka.[3] More than a thousand tourists from China came to Japan to enjoy the long Chinese New Year holidays to avoid the proliferation of COVID-19 in their country. The tweet has been retweeted and "liked" by over 60,000 twitter accounts in just one day. Some of them left hateful comments on the tweet such as "stop bringing the virus weapon to Japan," "ban them from entering (Japan)," and "go back (to China) now."[4]

This chapter is a survey on the impact of COVID-19 on Yokohama Chinatown and does not pretend to be comprehensive. It aims to see how the ethnic Chinese in the Chinatown community responded to the pandemic in order to sustain the Chinatown businesses and keep them afloat. From the authors' archive-based research, we found out that Yokohama Chinatown did not rebuild the community entirely on their own. In fact, the community bonding between overseas Chinese residents in the Chinatown and mainstream Japanese society is strong and most of the time the two groups work hand-in-hand in organizing activities and campaigns for the same purposes: to make Yokohama lively again and to attract visitors to experience the clean and safe Yokohama. At the point of writing, the fifth virus wave looms over Tokyo just two weeks before the start of the Tokyo Olympics. This writing collects information from online

---

[2] "Due to Coronavirus, Chinese are Banned from Entering the Shop," *Asahi Shimbun Digital*, accessed 3 August 2021, available at https://www.asahi.com/articles/ASN1P6Q80N1PULOB02D.html?iref=pc_photo_gallery_breadcrumb.

[3] "News on COVID-19 is Widely Spread on the Internet, Seek for Advice from Experts," *Nishi Nippon News*, accessed 3 August 2021, available at https://www.nishinippon.co.jp/item/n/580673/.

[4] *Ibid.*

material and reveals how Yokohama Chinatown is trying to survive during the pandemic period in the following manner: putting new business models into practice and continuous cooperation among restaurants and shops within the Chinatown and participating in community-wide activities and campaigns with its neighboring districts.

COVID-19 Coronavirus Pandemic and Yokohama Chinatown

Yokohama Chinatown stands out as a historical landmark icon of local community history of the largest Chinatown in Japan. The Chinatown was first established in the 1850s as a self-help community among the ethnic Chinese residents who were not allowed to live outside the area. The "Three Knives" (occupational terms meaning "scissor for tailor," "cleaver for chef," and "razor for barber") occupations were the major businesses that sustained the early Chinatown's business activities. Before the end of WWII in 1945, Yokohama Chinatown was a community that served the needs of the overseas Chinese in Japan. Since China, a member of the Allies in WWII, received better food supplies after the War, Japanese residents started the visit the Chinatown for food, and it marked the beginning of Yokohama Chinatown as a food and beverage (F&B) business-oriented community in Japan. Before the COVID-19 outbreak in Japan, Yokohama Chinatown hosted over 500 restaurants and shops within the ethnic quarter.

Yokohama Chinatown is the first district in Japan to be highlighted or "criticized" by some uninformed segments of the society. Since the first COVID-19 infected patient was confirmed to be ethnic Chinese from Kanagawa prefecture, some public perceptions tended to link up the ethnic Chinese resident in Japan with Chinatown in the early days of confusion over the outbreak, especially since both are located in the same prefecture. Yokohama Chinatown is then portrayed by some uninformed individuals as an area that is filled with large number of ethnic Chinese, who might have been in touch with COVID-19 inflected patients from Mainland China. Based on this misperception, some Japanese visitors avoided visiting Yokohama Chinatown ever since the first confirmed case appeared in Japan in January 2020. Takahashi Nobumasa, the chairperson of Yokohama Chinatown Development Association, was disappointed by the misleading information and fake news that came out from some

Japanese mass media outlets. Some Japanese media claimed that the Chinatown would be visited by many tourists from Mainland China for Lunar New Year celebration, which Takahashi pointed out was not true. Takahashi claimed, "95% of the visitors [to the Chinatown] are Japanese local tourists instead of mainland Chinese visitors. In fact, mainland Chinese visitors seldom visit Yokohama Chinatown for new year celebration."[5] A good evidence to show how Japanese visitors are avoiding Yokohama Chinatown is the rapid drop of Japanese mass media interview requests. Before COVID-19, Yokohama Chinatown Development Association usually received about 80–100 media interview requests on the Chinese New Year celebration events. But, with the coronavirus outbreak, many Japanese media refused to report the events and they did not encourage Japanese visitors to come to Yokohama Chinatown.[6]

The Lunar New Year celebration on 25 January 2020 was the first public large-scale event held within Yokohama Chinatown. According to Chinese traditions, the lunar New Year celebration starts with lion dance parade along the streets. Due to the COVID-19 coronavirus outbreak in Kanagawa prefecture, many restaurants and shops were largely affected financially due to the rapid decrease of visitors. Some ethnic Chinese shop owners even offered free face masks to visitors to show how the ethnic Chinese in the Chinatown are aware of the pandemic.[7] Nearly 500 restaurants and shops set up sanitizer facilities at their store-fronts for visitors to use for free.[8] Unfortunately, these measures did not bring much confidence to the Japanese consumers, and at least four Chinese restaurants in Yokohama Chinatown even received threatening letters from the misinformed. *Kaiinkaku*, a Cantonese restaurant operating since 1936, received a letter with content "Chinese people are trash! Bacteria! Devil! Trouble! Get out of Japan quickly!" printed in red color on 4 March 2020.[9] Similar

[5] "Coronavirus and the Harsh Condition of Yokohama Chinatown," *Toyo Keizai*, accessed 3 August 2021, available at https://toyokeizai.net/articles/-/334894?page=2.

[6] *Ibid.*

[7] "Chinatown in Chinese New Year. Shops that Offer Free Mask Believe It's Safe," *Asahi Shimbun Digital*, accessed 3 August 2021, available at https://www.asahi.com/articles/ASN1T5VXCN1TUTIL007.html?iref=pc_ss_date_article.

[8] *Ibid.*

[9] "A Few Restaurants in Yokohama Chinatown Received Hateful Letter. Please Stop," *Asahi Shimbun Digital*, accessed 3 August 2021, available at https://www.asahi.com/articles/ASN35641VN35ULOB007.html?iref=pc_photo_gallery_bottom.

letters were sent to a few other Chinese restaurants in Tokyo (Ueno or Shinagawa).[10] Not only restaurants, Yokohama Chinatown Development Association also received threatening phone calls and letters as well.[11] The anti-Chinese sentiments within Yokohama Chinatown continues to grow until today.

BuzzFeed News interviewed restaurant owner Lai from *Tōchinmi* on 12 March 2020. Lai told *BuzzFeed* that, although he thinks Yokohama Chinatown is now the safest place because of all the measures taken to maintain good hygiene, the number of customers has dropped rapidly starting from January 2020.[12] "Although there is no COVID-19 confirmed cases in Yokohama Chinatown, it is sad to see how people think the Chinatown is a terrible place," said Lai.[13] Lai received calls for cancellation of bookings, and compared to the same month in 2019 year-on-year, the business of *Tōchinmi* has dropped over 80%.[14] Seeing a number of Chinese restaurants closed down, or are considering to close temporarily, Lai promised not to lay off any of the employees because "they all have families to take care of" and "will not close *Tōchinmi*" even if he needs to apply for bank loan.[15]

Yokohama Chinatown Responses to COVID-19

F&B and retail businesses of Yokohama Chinatown have been greatly affected by the rapid drop of the number of visitors. Up till January 2021 (one year since the first COVID-19 inflected case emerged in Japan), more than 40 restaurants have closed down. In response to the situation, Yokohama Chinatown Development Association implemented different measures to restore confidence in visiting Yokohama Chinatown. Starting from March 2020, Yokohama Chinatown Development Association kicked off the entire campaign with the theme "#Ganbare Chūkagai" (literally translated as 'Hang in there Chinatown'):

---

[10] *Ibid.*

[11] *Ibid.*

[12] "The Talk and Sadness of Restaurant that Only Have One Customer, the Chinatown is the Safest Place Now," *BuzzFeedNews*, accessed 3 August 2021, available at https://www.buzzfeed.com/jp/kensukeseya/yokohama-chinatown-jiayou.

[13] *Ibid.*

[14] *Ibid.*

[15] *Ibid.*

> "#Ganbare Chūkagai" is a term that represents various support activities for Yokohama Chinatown against the impact of the new coronavirus. Yokohama Chinatown Development Association will devise support measures for visitors as well as union members (restaurants and shops) on the continuous economic activities. Also, to show support to the Yokohama City, Yokohama Chinatown Development Association will take as much social responsibility as possible to revitalize the city of Yokohama and the Chinatown.[16]

According to the official statement made by the Yokohama Chinatown Development Association, the entire "#Ganbare Chūkagai" campaign shows support to the community by revitalizing the local businesses. The Association provides many kinds of support, including financial support to their members (restaurants and shops in the Chinatown).[17] This campaign is supported by a number of well-known and large-scale Japanese corporations, including the likes of Asahi Beer, Itoen, Avex Group, Kirin Beers, Coca Cola Japan, Suntory, Soft Bank, Mitsui Fudosan, Mitsubishi Estate, and Keikyu Corporation.[18]

The hashtag on "#Ganbare Chūkagai" represents the utilization of this campaign slogan on social media. Because of serious misleading and even harassment messages on Yokohama Chinatown and the spread of coronavirus discrimination found on social media platforms, Yokohama Chinatown Development Association encourages the general public to use the hashtag "#がんばれ中華街" on social media, especially on Twitter feed where the hateful messages proliferated, and on any postings related to the Yokohama Chinatown. From March to December 2020, more than 200 posts were found on Twitter using the hashtag. Netizens usually use this hashtag in their comments toward the Chinese food in Yokohama Chinatown, or on the tagged photos of their visit to the Chinatown. Among these posts, many netizens showed their sympathies toward the businesses of Yokohama Chinatown. For example, Twitter user @jaydash2 took a picture of the empty Chinatown and the entrance of the closed restaurants on 21 September 2020. He used the hashtag "#がんば

[16] "Thank You Very Much for Supporting the #Ganbare Chūkagai Campaign," *Yokohama Chinatown*, accessed 3 August 2021, available at https://www.chinatown.or.jp/info/thankseveryone/.

[17] *Ibid.*

[18] *Ibid.*

れ中華街" when mentioning how empty Yokohama Chinatown was during the 3-day consecutive public holiday.[19] Another Twitter user @Paciorekjpn left a cheerful message to Yokohama Chinatown using the same hashtag after his visit to one of the Chinese restaurants in Yokohama Chinatown, *Hisuirō*, and felt pity for the restaurant.[20] Months after the pandemic has passed, some of the netizens began to show sympathy toward Yokohama Chinatown because, until the point of this writing, there is no more COVID-19 confirmed cases from the Chinatown. Twitter user @dcudgpcpj asked people to ignore those hateful and evidence-less comments toward Yokohama Chinatown.[21] He also used the hashtag in his post by mentioning that he would visit the Chinatown for food when the pandemic ends.

Thereafter, the Japanese broadcasting companies picked up their support to Yokohama Chinatown by using the same hashtag on their promotional posts of the TV program regarding Yokohama or Kanagawa prefecture. TV broadcasting company J:COM's tv program "In response to SOS! Local shopping" introduced Yokohama Chinatown in Episode 7, and the promotional post on J:COM official Twitter account used the hashtag "#がんばれ中華街" and claimed that the television broadcasted program aimed to support restaurants and shops in Yokohama Chinatown that were in financial difficulties due to COVID-19.[22] With the influence of mass media, some of the Japanese changed their mindset toward Yokohama Chinatown. The ethnic quarter is no longer as dangerous as they might have thought in the past, and some of them wrote their sympathies toward Yokohama Chinatown on Twitter after watching TV broadcasted programs about the Yokohama Chinatown. Twitter user @cocoa1004v posted her comment on Yokohama Chinatown after watching a TV program on 20 September 2020. From her point of view, it is not appropriate to link Yokohama Chinatown and COVID-19 coronavirus together because Chinese residents form the majority residents in the

---

[19] Jaydash. *Twitter Post*, 21 September 2020, 8:29 AM, available at https://twitter.com/jaydash2/status/1307839388521361408.

[20] Paciorekjpn. *Twitter Post*, 22 September 2020, 10:53 AM, available at https://twitter.com/Paciorekjpn/status/1308237981640134656.

[21] Dcudgpcpj. *Twitter Post*, 12 September 2020, 6:31 AM, available at https://twitter.com/dcudgpcpj/status/1304548144273735680.

[22] Jcom_info. *Twitter Post*, 12 June 2020, 8:59 AM, available at https://twitter.com/jcom_info/status/1271245730158571522.

ethnic quarter.[23] In fact, there is no evidence on how Yokohama Chinatown has direct connection with the spread of coronavirus in Japan.[24] After watching the TV program, @cocoa1004v started to worry about how restaurants and shops continue their business during this tough period.

Not only focusing on online promotion, Yokohama Chinatown Development Association utilized the tagline "#Ganbare Chūkagai" as the official slogan in the Chinatown. The Association organized an event on 20 March 2020 at *Zenrinmon* (one of the 10 gates in Yokohama Chinatown), and a large banner was placed at the front of the gate. *Zenrinmon* was first built in 1955 as the symbol of Yokohama Chinatown. The name means to "be friendly with neighbors" with a blessing to the Chinatown. The current *Zenrinmon* is the second one built in 1989. The message printed on the banner is "Thank you everyone! #Ganbare Chūkagai."[25] The Association expressed their grateful feelings to all visitors who chose to visit Yokohama Chinatown when the area became unpopular during the pandemic period. Nevertheless, the banner also acts as a cheer to the restaurants and shops in Yokohama Chinatown. Indeed, Yokohama Chinatown Development Association has been providing various support to the restaurants and shops in the area, including urgent financial support, setting up of consultancy center, providing COVID-19-related news and organizing public seminars on public health.[26] With this banner with the message of "#Ganbare Chūkagai," the Association hopes to remind the restaurants and shops that they are there to assist all members to go through this difficult period.

Although the COVID-19 pandemic brings more harm than good, the tough situation is also a good time for businesses to start thinking of new business models. Yokohama Chinatown sets a good example. Before the coronavirus spread widely in Japan, the Chinatown was famous for its dine-in service, especially the all-you-can-eat style, and "*tabearuki*" (eating while strolling). To reduce the number of customers in the restaurants, 31 restaurants offer take-out service and 9 restaurants have started

---

[23] Cocoa1004v. *Twitter Post*, 21 September 2020, 12:59 PM, available at https://twitter.com/cocoa1004v/status/1307907208181506049.

[24] *Ibid.*

[25] "Yokohama Chinatown Zenrinmon's Banner #Ganbare Chūkagai, Thank You Very Much Everyone," *Yokohama Keizai Shimbun*, accessed 3 August, 2021, available at https://www.hamakei.com/headline/10826/.

[26] *Ibid.*

delivery services, and more than 20 restaurants used Uber Eats Japan delivery service.[27] Yokohama Chinatown Development Association helps these restaurants to promote on the Chinatown official website. Not only does the Association listed out the name and address of these restaurants but they also packaged these delivery and take-out services as a part of the "#Ganbare Chūkagai" campaign and offer a prominent banner titled "Enjoy Yokohama Chinatown at Home" on the front-page of the website. Moreover, to increase customers' confidence to use take-out and delivery service in Yokohama Chinatown, the Association especially highlights the hygiene information of each restaurant at the remark column. For example, *Kantonhanten* (Guangdong restaurant), which provides take-out services, requires all staff to wear face mask. All containers are well-sanitized with alcohol, and all foods are handled with masked up staff with hand gloves. *Jyukeihanten*, on the other hand, requires all staff to submit health check proof every day before work. All dishes are freshly made and are recommended for consumption within two hours.[28]

Although the F&B sector is leading this new major business model in Yokohama Chinatown, Yokohama Chinatown Development Association did not neglect the business needs of the retail shops. Due to the spread of COVID-19 coronavirus in Japan, not only did the visitors avoided dining out but they also avoided walking along the streets of Yokohama Chinatown. The retail shops in Yokohama Chinatown, like restaurants, are in serious financial difficulties. The Association encourages its retail shop members to set up websites as a new e-platform and marketing channels to sell the products. Utilizing the same principles in the promotion of food take-outs and delivery services, "Enjoy Yokohama Chinatown at home" campaign introduces online retail shops in the Chinatown and encourage visitors to shop online. *Genhōkō*, a Chinese grocery store with over 70 years of history in Yokohama Chinatown, promises same-day delivery for all orders placed before noon.[29] In the online platform of Chinese handicrafts and paintings shop *Kaiunfusuihanamojya* visited by pre-pandemic Japanese visitors who wanted to have their Japanese names written in Chinese-style painting, visitors are able to place customized online orders without visiting the Chinatown during the pandemic.

---

[27] "#Ganbare Chūkagai Enjoy Yokohama Chinatown at Home!!" *Yokohama Chinatown*, accessed 3 August 2021, available at https://www.chinatown.or.jp/feature/takeout.

[28] *Ibid.*

[29] *Ibid.*

On 20 September 2020, a documentary named "Coronavirus and Chinatown: I Live with This Town" has broadcasted in a TV program series *The Nonfiction* produced by Fuji TV.[30] The one-hour documentary is based on a one-month observation study and interviews with the family members who own and operate a Chinese restaurant *Ryuhou* in Yokohama Chinatown. *Ryuhou* is opened by the second-generation Liang couple in 1980. Before COVID-19, *Ryuhou* was visited by many of the local Chinese residents as well as Japanese visitors for its famous crab fried rice dishes. Similar to other Chinese restaurants, with the decrease in number of local visitors, the restaurant have begun to sell take-out lunch boxes. Liang's daughter Ikuei delivers lunch boxes to the customers who live in the neighborhood. As many regular customers are elderly living alone by themselves, Ikuei visits them one by one to deliver their daily lunch boxes by bicycling to their residences. Also, it was the first time for the restaurant to accept take-out orders by LINE, a freeware app for instant communications that is popular in Japan. The Liang family sets an example showing how the Chinese restaurant copes with the impacts bought about by the pandemic. Changes needed to be implemented to meet with the needs of the "new daily life" — to provide take-out services, delivery services and make good use of communication apps on their mobile phone for their business activities.

Besides the measures carried out by the Chinese restaurants and retail shops, Yokohama Chinatown Development Association also organized a series of events to support the businesses of the Chinatown. Yokohama Chinatown is famous for its Chinese traditional rituals, such as lion, dragon, and other Chinese traditional dances during the celebration of Lunar New Year (also known as the Chinese New Year), Mid-autumn festival, and the Chinese National Day. Especially in the case of the lion dance, which carries the meaning of bringing good luck to the household and driving away the evil spirits, the performance is a "must-have" event for all Chinese festivals. Although these traditional Chinese rituals are not new to the local visitors, since the COVID-19 outbreak in Japan, Yokohama Chinatown Development Association once again utilized the traditional ritual to attract visitors to come to the Chinatown by giving them an additional service in performing the "function" of driving away the coronavirus. On 21 June 2020, Yokohama Chinatown worked

[30] "The Nonfiction," *Fuji TV*, accessed 3 August 2021, available at https://www.fujitv.co.jp/thenonfx/_basic/backnumber/index-67.html.

hand-in-hand with Kobe Chinatown in organizing a lion dance blessing event. Both Chinatowns showed support to each other by hosting a live broadcast on Facebook and sharing their visual materials on each other's Facebook page. At 3 pm, two lions, one yellow and one blue, paraded along the entrance of Yokohama Chinatown. They performed for about 10 minutes in accordance with the traditional ritual practice, which was meant to bring about good luck and fortune. The event attracted the nearby local visitors to spend time to watch the lion dance. A 54-year-old Japanese visitor was interviewed by *The Sankei News* and expressed his happiness in seeing the Chinatown becoming lively again.[31] Another local visitor, a 37-year-old Japanese office lady told *Yomiuri News* she gained spiritual courage from the lion dance performance after seeing how the Chinese worked hard on reviving the community.[32]

The communitarian and groupist collective atmosphere of the Chinatown was visible in these events. Furthermore, the activities are an effective collective mobilization of the stakeholders in the district by involving more than 500 restaurants and shops within Yokohama Chinatown, out of which more than 400 of them are the members of Yokohama Chinatown Development Association. The Association cares about the business sustainability of each member during COVID-19. Takahashi, the Chairperson of the Association, decided to enhance the #Ganbare Chūkagai campaign by adding new element and named it "kao wo mieru machi" (town where you can see the faces (of its stakeholders)) in March 2021.[33] Takahashi suggests introducing the people who supported the development of Yokohama Chinatown, including chefs, shop owners, and staff, to the public because most of the posts regarding Yokohama Chinatown on social media are about food and stakeholders at the street level. "If we [Yokohama Chinatown Development Association] introduce the people who are working hard to support the Chinatown, it

---

[31] "The Wish of the Suspension of COVID-19 of Lion Dance in Yokohama Chinatown," *The Sankei News*, accessed 3 August 2021, available at https://www.sankei.com/article/20200623-LHQNQEVHIFIHLPUBEBJNF7I7KQ/.

[32] "The Wish of the Suspension of COVID-19. Lion Dance from Yokohama Chinatown," *Yomiuri Shimbun*, accessed 3 August 2021, available at https://www.yomiuri.co.jp/national/20200621-OYT1T50166/.

[33] "The Rapid Drop of Number of Visitors, Challenge of Yokohama Chinatown," *Asahi Shimbun Digital*, accessed 3 August 2021, available at https://www.asahi.com/articles/ASP3275F8P2SULOB018.html.

will help to build up a closer relationship between the visitors and the people in the Chinatown," said Takahashi in an interview with *Asahi Shimbun*.[34] The "kao wo mieru machi" (literally translated as "the town or district with visible faces" similar to the "humans of" campaign like "the humans of Chinatown") is a social media campaign. The crew from Yokohama Chinatown Development Association visited its 400 plus member restaurants and shops, interviewed their representatives (usually chefs or owners), taped it, and uploaded the video on Youtube for public viewing. For example, chef Takatani from *Seikōen* in Yokohama Chinatown was asked about his recommended dishes, his career path as a Chinese chef in the Chinatown and his feelings toward the impact of COVID-19.[35] These videos emphasized human voices and emotions. Through these interview videos, the Association hopes to introduce Yokohama Chinatown to the visitors, and, more importantly, to let the public to understand the hardship of the stakeholders in the Chinatown who are still suffering from the pandemic. With the decline in the number of mass media interview requests from a peak of over 200 in 2019 to only 50 in 2020, Takahashi hopes that these videos can be a new channel to showcase the best of Yokohama Chinatown.[36]

Last but not least, Yokohama Chinatown Development Association seeks opportunities to work with Japanese corporations in bringing businesses to the Chinatown. A large Japan F&B service provider Suntory organized a support campaign "Sakimeshi" for the restaurants in Japan. "Sakimeshi" is a support project for restaurants by paying for the meal before you dine. The logic behind this campaign is that, because of the COVID-19 people are not going out as often, customers can buy the dining ticket of their choice of restaurant and dine at the restaurant after the end of the pandemic. The advantage of this project is that the restaurants can get the profits from dining ticket purchases instantly and use the money to overcome financial difficulties brought about by the COVID-19 coronavirus pandemic. With the tagline "although we cannot meet now, we are connected," the "Sakimeshi" attracted 44 restaurants from Yokohama Chinatown to join the project.[37]

---

[34] *Ibid.*

[35] *Ibid.*

[36] *Ibid.*

[37] "#Ganbare Chūkagai Enjoy Yokohama Chinatown at Home!!" *Yokohama Chinatown*, accessed 3 August 2021, available at https://www.chinatown.or.jp/feature/takeout.

Conclusion: Yokohama Chinatown in the Near Future

At the point of writing, there are only two weeks left before the beginning of Tokyo Olympics on 23 July 2021. The COVID-19 coronavirus is still a major issue affecting the daily lives of the Japanese. Tokyo is experiencing the fifth wave of Delta variant infections at the point of this writing, and the Tokyo government has announced the state of emergency from 12 July to 22 August 2021. With over 1,000 infected cases reported in for five consecutive days from 14 July in Tokyo alone, the government encourages the residents to stay home and avoid going out for leisurely visits. Being the neighboring region to the city of Tokyo, visitors avoided visiting Kanagawa prefecture during this critical pandemic period. This was self-restraint on the part of the Tokyoites as infection rates were the highest in their city and many followed the government's persuasion and advice to not travel outside Tokyo. COVID-19 might remain a challenging issue in Japan and the world, but it is also important to learn how to live with the virus in the future.

C Square Yokohama by Noge Printing is a video and website designer house in Yokohama. The company invites partners in Yokohama, including Yokohama Chinatown Development Association, to work on a project named "Wait for the Light." "Wait for the Light" means to hope for the best in the future: although it still is dark, there will be light again eventually.[38] The city of Yokohama is in the similar scenario as COVID-19 drives away the visitors and some of the retail and restaurant businesses in the city is in danger financially. C Square Yokohama by Noge Printing offers their free design expertise and platform on their website for this project, and they helped to create individual videos for each partner. In the 3-minute video on Yokohama Chinatown, the Chairperson of Yokohama Chinatown Development Association spent the first half of the interview in explaining how Yokohama Chinatown was criticized by netizens on social media when the first COVID-19 case was confirmed in January 2020 and the first community to be significantly affected by the pandemic in Japan.[39] However, although most of the business owners in

---

[38] "Project of Wait for the Light," *C Square Noge Printing*, accessed 3 August 2021, available at https://c-square.noge-printing.jp/wait_for_the_light/.

[39] "Wait for the Light Chapter 04 Yokohama Chinatown," *Youtube*, accessed 3 August 2021, available at https://www.youtube.com/watch?v=6vT3xdWKIPk&t=3s.

Yokohama Chinatown felt depressed and disappointed, when they read the positive and cheerful comments posted on twitter or other social media, they are very happy and thankful to the visitors who show support to the Chinatown. Therefore, Takahashi explained in the video that he would like to express his thanks for the support from the visitors by putting up a large banner at the gate of Yokohama Chinatown with tagline "Thank You Everyone!" as a part of the "#Ganbare Chūkagai" campaign.[40]

To live together with coronavirus, which the Japanese government encourages the public to live the "new daily life," requiring a new set of lifestyle. This also applies to businesses that are keen to operate as normal, and new business models are important to help sustain the businesses in the seeming endless pandemic waves. In the case of Yokohama Chinatown, the traditional Chinese restaurants (many of them has over 50 or more years of history) have taken one step forward to adapt to the new business model of operating semi-normally with restrictions in place and a heightened awareness of state of emergency coping mechanisms. As mentioned earlier in the chapter, some of the restaurants started to take delivery order through the mobile app LINE, which has never happened before in the past when it comes to the business operations of these old restaurants before the era of COVID-19 coronavirus pandemic. Indeed, a new pandemic-era business model has been established and operated in the Chinatown since 2020 — such as the drive-thru or/and take-out services. 33 Chinese restaurants in Yokohama Chinatown offer a special menu for "drive-thru" and/or take-out services, and from 11 am to 2 pm, these restaurants take orders by phone calls, and they deliver the dishes to the carpark near the North gate of Yokohama Chinatown. The "drive thru, take-out service" is organized and fully supported by Yokohama Chinatown Development Association. They negotiated with different parties, especially the North Gate carpark because most of the streets are pedestrian-only access and North Gate carpark is the most convenient and spacious area for the services rendered. The "drive thru, take-out" service cannot take place without collective contribution and support from the community. This new business model reveals the unity and cohesion of the overseas Chinese community in Yokohama Chinatown, and set a good example to see how the community associations can work hand-in-hand

[40] *Ibid.*

with businesses to set up new business model to cope with the "new daily life" reality.

It is important to note that "Wait[ing] for the light" is not a passive attitude. In fact, positive action has to be taken in order to see the "light" (perhaps comparable to the allusion to the English phrase "light at the end of the tunnel"). For Yokohama Chinatown, the Yokohama Chinatown Development Association encourages all owners and staff to get vaccinated in order to restore public confidence in the retail district back to the public and invite them back to visit the Chinatown. The Chairperson Takahashi told NHK News that organizing large-scale vaccination program is a way to show the public how safe Yokohama Chinatown is.[41] More than 4,300 people who work in the Chinatown are scheduled to get vaccinated on 28 July 2021.[42] COVID-19 has been a continuous nightmare to Yokohama Chinatown. Due to the strains of repeated states of emergency, it may not be surprising to see more restaurants and shops in Yokohama Chinatown close down in near future. No one is able to tell when the "light" will finally be able to be seen at the end of the tunnel. But, with the new measures and business models, cooperation within the overseas Chinese community, and support from mainstream Japanese society, someday Yokohama Chinatown will be lively again.

---

[41] "Vaccine Program at Workplace in Yokohama Chinatown," *Town News*, accessed 3 August 2021, available at https://www.townnews.co.jp/0113/2021/07/01/580988.html.
[42] *Ibid.*

https://doi.org/10.1142/9789811253737_0005

Chapter 5

The Resilience of Hong Kong's Civil Society under COVID-19 Conditions

Ka Shing Ng

Background

Hong Kong is one of the East Asian regional areas that has succeeded relatively well in containing the COVID-19 coronavirus pandemic in its early stages. While this can be partly attributed to the measures promptly implemented by the Hong Kong government, the role of its civil society in responding to the crisis should not be underestimated. Especially during the early outbreak, when the government was unable to solve the mask shortage problem effectively, many interested individuals and groups had taken the lead to secure mask supplies. This chapter examines the role of Hong Kong's civil society in the fight against the pandemic with a focus on the mask issue. It starts with an overview of the pandemic in Hong Kong and discusses some of the factors that have helped Hong Kong contain the outbreak as compared to other regions. By focusing on the mask shortage crisis during the early outbreak, I argue that one of the most important factors behind the so-called Hong Kong's "COVID-19 success story" (Leader League, 2020) is the resilience of Hong Kong's civil society. Due to travel restrictions, the author has not been able to conduct field studies in Hong Kong. Therefore, the data presented in this chapter are mainly based on textual materials collected online, such as news articles, government press releases, activity reports released by NGOs, etc.

COVID-19 Measures in Hong Kong

Compared to the US and most European countries, some East Asian societies have done a good job in dealing with the COVID-19 pandemic, with Taiwan, Hong Kong, and Singapore, for example, maintaining a relatively low number of infection and fatality well below the world's average (Worldometers, 2021). In Hong Kong, since the first case was confirmed on 23 January 2020, the number of new cases per day had remained low (approximately 10 cases) until the first wave of the pandemic erupted in late March 2020. Subsequent outbreaks were observed between July and September 2020 (second wave), November 2020 and early January 2021 (third wave), and in late January 2021 (fourth wave), and at the time of this writing in March 2021, Hong Kong is hit by the fifth wave. Despite occasional outbreaks, Hong Kong has so far been able to keep infections and deaths low. As of 16 March 2021, the total number of cases is 11,330 and deaths 203 (Hong Kong SAR Government, 2021). These figures can be considered relatively low given the high population density of this small city. This has earned Hong Kong worldwide recognition with some mass media outfits saying, for example, "Hong Kong's success against COVID-19" is a "tutorial for India and the world" (Jacob, 2020) and "Hong Kong beat coronavirus and avoided lockdown" (Saiidi, 2020). I suggest the following four measures are keys to containing the outbreak in Hong Kong during the early stage.

Suspension of school and call for mask-wearing at an early stage

Only two days after the first case was confirmed on 23 January 2020, the government promptly announced the activation of "Emergency Response Level" and implemented measures to tackle the virus (Hong Kong Government, 2020a). To prevent outbreak in local community, not only large-scale events like the Chinese New Year Carnival and the Lunar New Year Cup football tournament were canceled, but school classes were also suspended to lower the risk of virus infection in schools. These measures have helped prevent the formation of infection clusters in the local community. As the situations seemed to get better in May 2020, the government decided to resume classes incrementally but remained cautious about the developments of the pandemic. Some primary and secondary schools have also begun to move their classes online, as plans for the resumption of schools have been constantly interrupted by further outbreaks. Universities have also switched their classes to an online basis since January 2020. The suspension of school at the outset of the pandemic has been crucial for minimizing local infection.

Besides, Hong Kong citizens have been quick enough to adopt the mask-wearing habit as a preventive measure against the virus since January 2020. It should be noted that, however, the Hong Kong government seemed reluctant to promote this practice at the very beginning. Many critics suggested that such passive attitudes toward mask-wearing is related to the anti-mask law emergently enacted by the government in October 2019 to crackdown mass protests. While the government remained indecisive about whether to endorse the use of face masks by the public, some infection preventionists and experts, based on their professional judgments, came out and encouraged the public to wear masks as a key measure to prevent infections. Their advice was later accepted by the government and wearing face masks in the public has soon become a new normal in Hong Kong. Since July 2020, the government has made wearing faces in public areas compulsory; maximum penalty for breaching this measure is a HKD10,000 fine.

Strict quarantine measures

As early as 5 February 2020, the Hong Kong government required all individuals traveling from the Chinese mainland to Hong Kong, regardless of nationality, to receive a 14-day stay-home quarantine. On 17 March 2020, the government further announced the highest level of travel alert and urged the public to avoid traveling to all countries and regions, except for Mainland China, Taiwan, and Macau. Moreover, people undergoing home quarantine were required to wear tracking wristbands to ensure they stayed in the designated areas. If found violating the regulations, they could face up to 6 months imprisonment and a HKD 25,000 fine. As the pandemic spread globally and confirmed cases among inbound travelers have continued to increase, quarantine measures have also been strengthened. For instance, people returning to Hong Kong from high risks places are required to receive compulsory quarantine for 21 days in designated hotels (Hong Kong Government, 2020b). As of March 2021, almost every country in the world has implemented similar quarantine measures. The risks posed by inbound travelers to Hong Kong have been largely minimized because the government was quick enough to implement and tighten quarantine measures in early February 2020 just before the global outbreak.

Partial closures of border

When the first case was confirmed on 23 January 2020, the government immediately shut down all the flights departing from Wuhan to Hong Kong. On 28 January, the government further announced a series of measures to restrict the movement of people between the Chinese mainland and Hong Kong, which included suspending some transportation services like flight, high-speed rail, ferry, and bus linking the mainland, and temporarily stopping the issue of tourist visas for mainlanders to Hong Kong. Since 25 March 2020, non-residents arriving at the Hong Kong airport have been denied entry; restrictions on transiting through Hong Kong have also been implemented.

Social distancing measures

Hong Kong is one of the regions that has introduced social distancing measures and been able to avoid extreme lockdown measures during the early outbreak. As early as 23 March 2020, the government announced the "alcohol ban" policy prohibiting the sale of alcoholic beverages in bars and restaurants, because "people tend to have intimate contact when consuming liquor," as explained by Carrie Lam, the Chief Executive of Hong Kong (Chan, 2020). However, the ban was lifted just after 4 days as the catering industry expressed strong concerns over its drastic effects on their business. The government then announced a new measure known as the "prohibition on group gathering" (aka. gathering ban) under which gatherings with more than 4 people would not be allowed. Also, the new measure requires restaurants to halve their seating and keep a 1.5-meter distance or above between tables. Some business and recreational facilities like cinemas and gyms were closed to prevent mass infection. Since the gathering ban was implemented, the number of people allowed in gatherings has been revised regularly based on the infection status at that time. For instance, the restriction on capacity was loosened to 8 people on 8 May and later to 50 on 19 June 2020. However, as Hong Kong was hit by the third wave in July with more than 100 new cases confirmed every day, the ban was tightened again to prohibit gatherings with more than 4 people. This reflects the "suppression and lift" approach to social distancing measures adopted by the government (Hong Kong Government, 2020c). "The novel coronavirus may not go away and we will have to learn to live with it and adapt to the new normal. The public should be prepared that small-scale local outbreaks are inevitable from time to time. Social distancing measures may need to be tightened at times," explained the government on its COVID-19 special webpage. In early 2021, to further minimize the risk of outbreak in local community, the government has begun to lockdown locations with discovered cases of COVID-19 for 48 hours.

Since the first case was confirmed in mid-January 2020, the Hong Kong government has reacted promptly by implementing the above measures, which have been vital to containing local outbreaks and minimizing risks posed by inbound travels during the early stage. The success of Hong Kong in dealing with the crisis can partly be attributed to the swift actions taken by the government.

Behind Hong Kong's "Success Story"

The above measures have proved to be effective in Hong Kong, but its "success story" is more than that. To better understand the "story," attention should also be paid to the social and political contexts of Hong Kong. Three important perspectives are keys to understanding the overall performance of Hong Kong during the pandemic, which are the prior SARS experience, Hong Kong people's distrust in the government, and the resilience of Hong Kong's civil society. In the following sections of the writing, the first two factors are discussed briefly followed by a more in-depth discussion of the third.

SARS experience

Hong Kong was able to respond in a fast manner largely due to the experience it gained during the deadly SARS pandemic in 2003. After the Chinese mainland, where the earliest identified cases were reported, Hong Kong was the second most affected region, with a total of 1,755 cases claiming 299 lives (Leung *et al.*, 2009). This tragic experience is a lesson for Hong Kong to formulate better systems and strategies in case of future outbreaks (Lai and Wai, 2010). There has also been an increasing awareness of health and hygiene among the public after SARS, which makes it easier for the government to implement anti-infection policies and for the citizens to promptly adopt prevention measures voluntarily during the early outbreaks of the COVID-19 pandemic. Another lesson Hong Kong people learned from SARS is the fact that virus has no border, and everyone is exposed to pandemic threats coming from all over the world. SARS first began in Guangdong province, China, and was transmitted by mainlander visitors to Hong Kong, where the global outbreak started (Xu *et al.*, 2004). This has served as a strong reminder for Hong Kong people that transborder risks, especially those coming from our geographically proximate neighbors, can potentially threaten our lives. Hong Kong people has since then maintained a high level of vigilance in terms of hygiene and disease prevention and control measures.

Distrust of government

When COVID-19 pandemic hit Hong Kong in January 2020, the city had just experienced its largest mass protests in history and people's distrust in the government remained high. According to the Hong Kong Public Opinion Research Institute (former Public Opinion Programme, the University of Hong Kong), the level of trust in government has been declining since the handover in 1997. As of July 1997, 12% of respondents claimed that they do not trust the government; the figure was hovering between 10% and 30% over the past 20 years (Hong Kong Public Opinion Research Institute, 1992–2021). However, when the anti-extradition protests broke out in June 2019, it surged to 60% and later reached its peak at 75.9% in February 2020. It means that the government had to deal with the pandemic in a challenging situation when public trust hit rock bottom. A few studies show people's discontent with government's measures in response to the epidemic. For example, according to a telephone survey conducted by the Hong Kong Institute of Asia-Pacific Studies of the Chinese University of Hong Kong (2020) in March 2020, over 70% of respondents said that the government's COVID-19 measures were "insufficient" or "very insufficient." Also, the same survey reveals that over 60% considered the performance of government in monitoring the epidemic "bad" or "very bad." Considering the chronological order of events, people's negative views on COVID-19 measures might partially reflect their distrust in the government for political reasons.

As distrust in the government pervaded, there has been increasing sentiments in Hong Kong society that people are left to deal with the pandemic by themselves (*Oriental Daily*, 2020). In early January 2020, the civil society and the business sector have taken the initiatives to procure and even manufacture face masks. A "new normal" of avoiding non-essential and non-urgent outings has been advocated from the bottom-up in society. Moreover, some companies have swiftly switched to work from home (WFH) in early February 2020. For example, a survey conducted by consulting firm Mercer (2020) revealed that 88% out of 300 companies interviewed in Hong Kong have already adopted WFH in February. Many companies have also suspended overseas business trips, distributed hand sanitizer and face masks to employees, and required those who have traveled to Mainland China to self-quarantine. One of the reasons why some companies were able to transit to WFH smoothly is that they had already explored alternative working styles back in June 2019 when traffic was occasionally disrupted by mass protests.

Resilience of Hong Kong's civil society

The power of civil society is one of the most important factors leading to Hong Kong's "success" in combating the pandemic. From the colonial era onward, Hong Kong's civil society has played a significant role in the development of social welfare and movements. A large part of education, medical, social welfare services have been provided and operated by NGOs and NPOs like secular charity groups and faith-based organizations. Many civil society organizations have also engaged in social and political activities like advocating democracy and human rights in Hong Kong. Since the early stages of the pandemic, the civil society in Hong Kong has already shown its effectiveness in various ways. For instance, hundreds of medical workers started a series of strikes in January 2020 when the government refused to close Hong Kong's border with Mainland China, which they argue could effectively minimize cases caused by inbound travelers. The government later announced the closure of more border crossings but insisted that this decision has nothing to do with the strikes (AFP, 2020). The actions of these medical workers, though condemned by Carrie Lam as "irrational," have further enhanced public awareness about the risks posed by the pandemic and the importance of stricter border controls.

One of the best examples showing the resilience of Hong Kong's civil society is its speedy and proactive actions in response to the mask shortage crisis during the early period of the pandemic. Even though medical experts had started to call on the public to wear masks to prevent the spread of infection in January 2020, the Hong Kong government remained passive in formulating mask policies, taking minimum actions in promoting the use of masks and securing mask supply for the public. As mentioned above, some critics argued that the government's reluctance to tackle the mask crisis is related to the anti-mask law enacted on 4 October 2019, which aimed to suppress the long-lasting protests triggered by the controversial extradition bill in June 2019. The law prohibited participants of mass protests and political gatherings from wearing face masks. The maximum penalty for violation is 1-year imprisonment and a fine of HKD 25,000. The outbreak of COVID-19 under the mask ban has presented an "embarrassing challenge" for the government. If it urged the public to wear face masks, then the mask ban just enacted 3 months ago would become *de facto* ineffective, undermining government's effort to crack-down the protests. It also meant that the government would have to withdraw the controversial anti-mask law with its own hands, which could further affect the credibility of the already unpopular government.

Therefore, many critics suspected that this is the reason why the government initially refrained from proactively endorsing the use of face masks. Some even criticized the government for formulating COVID-19 measures based on political considerations instead of science, sacrificing the welfare of Hong Kong citizens (*Ming Pao*, 2020). Without clear instructions regarding mask policies from the government, Hong Kong people were placed in a dilemma: wearing face masks to protect themselves from infection or not to do so under the "anti-mask law." They were left on their own to determine and choose between the risk of being infected or the risk of breaking the law. Under such circumstances, the civil society in Hong Kong showed strong resilience by taking the lead to deal with the mask crisis from a bottom-up approach, including securing mask supplies, providing correct information regarding the use of face masks, and even opening factories to manufacture masks locally.

In February 2020, the government finally accepted the advice from medical experts and began to promote the use of face masks as an effective measure to prevent the spread of COVID-19 infection.

However, even though the government became more positive to the use of face masks, it remained slow in formulating measures or policies to respond to the mask shortage crisis. In a press conference held on 8 February 2020, when asked what measures the government would take to tackle the mask problem, the Chief Executive Carrie Lam answered:

> There are 12 million masks currently in stock, which is enough to last about one month. But we should let those standing on the front line like staff members of the department of health to use the masks first. Also, I would like to ask those civil organizations and companies that are able to purchase masks to donate them to people in need, and to provide information on the sources of the masks to the government. (Chow and Tang, 2020)

Lam's response attracted strong public criticism, with many saying the government lacked the resolution and ability to solve the crisis. To restore public trust, the government released a statement on 20 February to clarify the measures it had taken to secure mask supply. It writes:

> For the supply of surgical masks, the Government has been adopting a multi-pronged approach to procure surgical masks globally through different channels and means. These include the Government Logistics Department procuring directly from suppliers and through referrals from the Hong Kong Economic and Trade Offices and from individual sources in order to secure the supply of masks and other protective items as soon as possible to meet the needs of the Government operation. (Hong Kong Government, 2020)

The government emphasized it is striving to procure surgical masks but it also iterated "meeting the needs of the Government operation" is the first priority. As for the public, the government preferred to stick to the *laissez-faire* principle to rely on the market to respond to the rising local demand for face masks.

> The Government is maintaining close contact with members of local chambers of commerce and the retail industry and collaborating with the Mainland Authorities to facilitate clearance so as to speed up their delivery to the market. [...] As the supply of surgical masks is tight in the short run, the Government considers that it is more pragmatic to strive

> to increase supply of surgical masks and manage the demand. The Government currently does not have any plans to mandatorily control the supply and prices of surgical masks through legislation, because this could be counterproductive, rather than addressing the problem at source, i.e. inadequate supply. (Hong Kong Government, 2020)

While face masks prices in Hong Kong rocketed under severe shortage, the government failed to come up with practical methods to cool down the market and make them affordable for ordinary people. Many working-class people and the elderly had difficulties purchasing face masks and were forced to reuse the old ones, making them vulnerable to infection. Caritas Hong Kong, the welfare service unity of the Catholic Church in Hong Kong, conducted a survey between February and March 2020 on the livelihood of low-income families in Hong Kong. Among the 309 households interviewed, 48.9% said they would run out of masks within two weeks and 52.8% said they would reuse old masks (Caritas Hong Kong, 2020). Also, 43% felt depressed because they could not afford to buy masks due to their financial difficulties.

As the government failed to tackle to mask crisis effectively, the question of how to maintain a stable and sufficient supply of masks has become an urgent issue for Hong Kong's civil society. Between January and February 2020, one of the most important actors in procuring face masks for Hong Kong people were shop owners and retailers. Owners of drug stores utilized their business networks to import masks from neighboring regions like Japan, South Korea, and Taiwan, as well as from Europe and India, when export restrictions on masks have not yet been exercised in these places during the early outbreak. This was made possible thanks to the fact that Hong Kong has long functioned as one of the most important entrepot and logistic centers in the world since its opening in the mid-19 century. The extensive trading networks formed between Hong Kong and the rest of the world help facilitated business exchanges even at the grass-root levels. In addition to shop owners, many independent retailers and parallel goods traders went to neighboring countries to purchase face masks and sterilizers directly, when overseas travel were not restricted, and then resell them in Hong Kong. However, as the pandemic spread globally in the end of February 2020, many countries began to shut down their borders as they faced a critical shortage of masks, making procuring face masks in this way extremely difficult, if not impossible.

Some readers may wonder why Hong Kong does not manufacture its own masks like other countries but has rely on sources overseas. It is because it lacks sufficient machines and factories required for the mass production of masks. Back in the 1960s to 1970s, Hong Kong's manufacturing industry once thrived, with goods like electronics and clothes carrying the label "Made in Hong Kong" that enjoyed high popularity among consumers around the world. However, since the opening of China in the late 1970s, many factory owners moved their production lines to the mainland for lower labor costs there. This not only led to the rapid decline of Hong Kong's manufacturing industry but also speeded up its transition to an international financial center. Due to the shift in economic structure, Hong Kong was inadequate in terms of manufacturing capacity for such PPE equipment and became highly dependent on the imports of foreign goods. Therefore, the procuring of face masks from sources overseas during the early outbreak of COVID-19 can be considered a consequence of Hong Kong's economic transition over the past few decades.

As the pandemic spread globally, many countries began to implement export restrictions on medical goods including face masks to meet rising local demand. Without a stable supply of masks, many Hong Kong people realized that they were confronted with a life and death problem. To find a way out of this crisis, some began to consider the possibility of manufacturing masks locally. For instance, Mr. Tang, a Hong Kong film producer, started up a mask factory with his friend in February 2020. They spent HKD 150,000 to purchase a mask-making machine from Chennai, India, which could produce 100,000 masks per day (*Reuters*, 2020). They also planned to purchase seven more machines by the end of April 2020 to meet the growing market demand for face masks in Hong Kong. In an interview with *Reuters*, Mr. Tang said:

> "I got angry looking for masks, they're either all sold out, or the masks that are from overseas are sold at an inflated price," Tang said, "wearing a mask, at the factory set up close to the border with the mainland. […] So I thought, making a mask isn't that hard, just some fabric sewn together, how about I make my own factory?" (Reuters, 2020)

Humanity is often tested in times of crisis. While there were some drug store owners with a selfless heart distributing free masks to people in need, there were also profit-oriented businessmen selling masks at high prices, with reports saying that a piece of mask was sold HKD10 at some shops. Angered by these profit-seekers, Mr. Tang said the masks they produce would cost only HKD1 each to ensure low-income families could also afford. The Hong Kong government has always been proud of its economic principle of *laissez-faire* to promote and sustain a free market. However, when masks price rocketed to the extent that so many people could not afford them, the government still refrained from intervening in the market, for example, by banning the resale of face mask at higher prices like the Japanese government did in March 2020 (*Mainichi*, 2020).

Another famous figure contributing to solve the mask crisis in Hong Kong is Dr. Kwong Si-san, who is an expert in Chemistry and had been teaching at university for a long time. His reaction was even faster than the government. In early January, when the news of unknown virus in Wuhan reached Hong Kong, Dr. Kwong has already started to share his professional knowledge on Facebook, teaching his online audience preventive measures like how to sterilize objects properly. As many people were not familiar with the differences in masks, he explained in plain language the level of protection different masks could offer. Also, when fake news about the virus and preventive measures spread in society, he created many poses on his Facebook to correct them and promote ways to combat with the pandemic based on scientific methods.

When the mask shortage problem was getting serious, Dr. Kwong, together with his friends, announced their plan to develop masks locally in the end of January. Their idea is to create a mask that is made of cloth with a filter fit into it. In this way, the DIY mask can be reused by washing the cloth part and replacing just the filter inside. After rounds of experiments and tests, they finally announced the HK Mask project on 21 February. In fact, they spent only three weeks from announcing their plan to officially releasing the final products. They were proud to name the mask HK Mask because the main components (cloth and filters) are made in Hong Kong, and, most importantly, the idea itself originated in Hong Kong. While the government was still baffled by the mask shortage problem, Dr. Kwong and his team had already taken actions to protect the lives of Hong Kong people. From this example, we can see the strong resilience of Hong Kong's civil society in times of crisis especially when the government failed to function properly.

The story of HK Mask was also widely reported by the Japanese media and quickly sparked a DIY mask boom in Japan. For instance, Kodansha's digital magazine *Friday* published an interview with Dr. Kwong in an article called "Hong Kong doctor urgently developed!

'I teach you how to make Corona mask'" on 25 March 2020 (*Friday Digital*, 2020). "We need masks that are cheap and safe. The manual for this DIY mask that I invented is also uploaded on the Internet. I want people in need use it," explained Dr. Kwong in the same interview (*Friday Digital*, 2020). The DIY HK Mask was one of the alternatives used by the people in Hong Kong and Japan when they were confronting a dire shortage of face masks. Also, "diseases do not care our political positions and they can affect anyone. I want to help Hong Kong with this mask regardless of 'yellow' (pro-democracy) or 'blue' (pro-government). I want to harmonize society with this mask," added Dr. Kwong when referring to the social and political unrest in Hong Kong (*Friday Digital*, 2020).

Apart from public-minded individuals like Mr. Tang and Dr. Kwong, the actions taken by civil organizations in response to the mask crisis have also been spectacular. In late-January 2020, a number of charitable groups and religious organizations started to distribute free masks especially to low-income people and promote preventive measures to increase public awareness for hygiene. To take religious groups as examples, the Christian community has played a significant role in dealing with the mask shortage. For instance, on 11 February, the Riviera Gardens Church of the Christian and Missionary Alliance distributed 8,000 masks to elderly people and medical staff (Ko, 2020). Kong Fuk Church of the Evangelical Free Church of China started the "care society, share masks" campaign, calling on their church members to donate spare face masks to other members and people in need. Good Neighbour North District Church organized the "protect our children, mask distribution activity" on 14 March, giving out masks to 200 secondary school and university students (Good Neighbour North District Church Facebook, 2020). Also, Caritas Hong Kong conducted a survey in February 2020 on the livelihood of low-incoming households, revealing the hardships they faced under the pandemic (Caritas Hong Kong, 2020). The survey helped increase public awareness and concern about the socially vulnerable groups and put pressure on the government to formulate relief measures for them.

In addition to the Christian community, the Buddhist and Taoist community also contributed to tackling the growing public demand for masks. On 10 February, the Hong Kong Buddhist Association, the Buddhist umbrella organization in Hong Kong, distributed face masks to kindergartens, schools, elderly homes and centers, low-income families, elderly people living alone, as well as people working in the cleaning services industry. Buddhist monks performed incantations on the masks before distributing, praying that Hong Kong would overcome this challenge and our lives could return to normal soon. Similarly, the Hong Kong Taoist Association also gave out masks and sterilizers to the public.

From the above examples, we can see that Hong Kong's civil society has shown high resilience to tackle the mask shortage problem, especially when the Hong Kong government failed to respond effectively to the crisis. This phenomenon is well described by the title of an article published by *Hong Kong Free Press* on 4 March 2020, which writes "Doing it ourselves: How Hongkongers innovate to tackle coronavirus shortages" (Chandra, 2020). In the article, the author rightly captures the resilience shown by Hong Kong's civil society when the systems that we have relied on have failed to function properly.

> […] civil society emerges as rapid response groups form when the usual parties responsible become stuck and paralysed. The outbreak has roused the entrepreneurial and innovative spirit of citizens as a means of resilience and survival. […] The gist of citizen innovation is that it is first and foremost not about profit. It is driven by solidarity, reciprocity, compassion for others, and trust. […]. (Chandra, 2020)

Wan and his colleagues also highlighted the power of community and social mobilization in the fight again COVID-19 in Hong Kong (Wan *et al*., 2020). In particular, they suggest the "strong and spontaneous mobilization" cite of local communities has been made possible due to the fact that Hong Kong people have experienced the SAR outbreak in 2003 and social movements in 2019. They also added that people's doubts about the policies of the government and WHO have facilitated the formation of "self-help model" in Hong Kong society. Perhaps, Hong Kong's civil society, which is characterized by a sense of solidarity, reciprocity, compassion for others, and trust (Chandra, 2020), is one of the important keys to combat the pandemic in Hong Kong.

Conclusion

Compared to its Western counterparts, Hong Kong has performed well during the early outbreak of the pandemic. This chapter suggested four important measures taken by the government have been effective in containing local infection, which included the suspension of school and call for mask-wearing, strict quarantine measures, partial closures of border, and social distancing measures. These measures have been implemented in a fast manner to prevent a region-wide outbreak in Hong Kong. However, in addition to the above measures, there are some important factors behind Hong Kong's "success story" that should not be underestimated. The first one is lessons from SARS, which improved the preparedness of Hong Kong's medical system for pandemics, as well as greatly increased the health and hygiene awareness of the public.

The second factor is the persistent decline of people's trust in the government, especially during and after the mass protests in 2019. This has fostered the formation of a sense of self-preservation in Hong Kong society. The idea that "Hong Kongers save themselves" (*Ming Pao Weekly*, 2020) has further strengthened the power of Hong Kong's civil society in response to social crisis. The third and also the most important factor, I argue, is the resilience of Hong Kong's civil society. When the mask shortage problem emerged during the early coronavirus breakout, ambitious individuals and charitable organizations acted promptly to procure face masks from overseas and even establishing factories to manufacture masks locally like HK Mask. Most of these masks were sold at affordable prices or distributed freely to people in need to ensure no one is left behind because of financial difficulties.

The COVID-19 pandemic has accentuated both the weaknesses and strengths of many countries. In the case of Hong Kong, the civil society, which has actively engaged in promoting the betterment of society, has also shown strong resilience in respond to the crisis. It also suggests a healthy and strong civil society is vital for managing risks for every society as the authority may sometimes fail.

References

AFP (2020). "Coronavirus: Hong Kong Shuts Most China Crossings over Virus as Medics Strike," *Hong Kong Free Press*, accessed 26 March 2021, available at https://hongkongfp.com/2020/02/03/coronavirus-hong-kong-medics-strike-govt-refuses-close-china-border/.

Caritas Hong Kong (2020). "Yiqing Xia Jiceng Jiating Chujing Wenjuan Diaocha (Survey on the Situation of Grassroots Families under the Epidemic)," accessed 26 March 2021, available at https://cd.caritas.org.hk/report/20200302.pdf.

Chan, Michelle (2020). "Hong Kong to Ban Liquor Sales at Bars and Restrict Visitor Arrivals," *Nikkei Asia*, accessed 26 March 2021, available at https://asia.nikkei.com/Spotlight/Coronavirus/Hong-Kong-to-ban-liquor-sales-at-bars-and-restrict-visitor-arrivals.

Chandra, Yanto. (2020). "Doing It Ourselves: How Hongkongers Innovate to Tackle Coronavirus Shortages," *Hong Kong Free Press*, accessed 26 March 2021, available at https://hongkongfp.com/2020/03/04/govt-fails-hongkongers-innovate-tackle-coronavirus-shortages/.

Chow, L. H. and Tang, K. K. (2020). "[Wuhan feiyan] Lin Zheng: Jing Gang ao Ban Cong Neidi Gou ru 1700 Wan Ge Kouzhao (Carrie Lam: Purchase 1.7 Million Masks from Mainland through Hong Kong and Macau Office of the State Council)," *HK01*, accessed 26 March 2021, available at https://www.hk01.com/%E6%94%BF%E6%83%85/432018.

Friday Digital (2020). "Honkon no Hakase ga Kinkyu Kaihatsu! "Koronamasuku no Tsukurikata, Oshiemasu" (Hong Kong Doctor Urgently Developed! I Teach You How To Make Corona Mask)," accessed 26 March 2021, available at https://friday.kodansha.co.jp/article/103421.

Good Neighbour North District Church (2020). "Poster," accessed 31 March 2020, available at https://www.facebook.com/GoodNeighbournd/posts/2242473562713673.

Hong Kong Government (2020). "Government Responds to Media Enquiries on Legislating on Mask Supply and Prices," accessed 26 March 2021, available at https://www.info.gov.hk/gia/general/202002/10/P2020021000639.htm.

Hong Kong Government (2020a). "CE Announces Activation of Emergency Response Level in Relation to Novel Coronavirus Infection," accessed 26 March 2021, available at https://www.info.gov.hk/gia/general/202001/26/P2020012600087.htm.

Hong Kong Government (2020b). "Points to Note for Quarantine for Inbound Travellers," accessed 9 September 2021, available at https://www.coronavirus.gov.hk/eng/inbound-travel.html.

Hong Kong Government (2020c). "Social Distancing," accessed 26 March 2021, available at https://www.coronavirus.gov.hk/eng/social_distancing.html.

Hong Kong Government (2021). "Latest Local Situation of COVID-19 (Details of Previous COVID-19 Cases)," accessed 26 March 2021, available at https://www.coronavirus.gov.hk/eng/index.html.

Hong Kong Institute of Asia-Pacific Studies of the Chinese University of Hong Kong (2020). "Survey Findings on Views about COVID-19," accessed 26 March 2021, available at https://www.cpr.cuhk.edu.hk/en/press/survey-findings-on-views-about-covid-19-released-by-hong-kong-institute-of-asia-pacific-studies-at-cuhk/.

Hong Kong Public Opinion Research Institute (1992–2021). "People's Trust in the HKSAR Government," accessed 9 September 2021, available at https://www.pori.hk/pop-poll/government-en/k001.html?lang=en.

Jacob, Rahul (2020). "Hong Kong's Success Against COVID-19: A Tutorial for India and the World," *Business Standard*, accessed 26 March 2021, available at https://www.business-standard.com/article/beyond-business/hong-kong-s-covid-19-tutorial-for-the-world-120041001350_1.html.

Ko, Sze Man (2020). "Xuandao Hui Haibin Tang Pai Kouzhao Yu 860 Ren Shou Huitang Zhuren Houyongyi: Xintu Ci Shi Ying Yan Huo Xinyang," *Christian Times*, accessed 26 March 2021, available at https://christiantimes.org.hk/Common/Reader/News/ShowNews.jsp?Nid=161188&Pid=102&Version=0&Cid=2186&Charset=big5_hkscs.

Lai, T. S. and Yu, W. C. (2010). "The Lessons of SARS in Hong Kong," accessed 26 March 2021, *Clinical Medicine* (London, England), 10(1), 50–53, available at https://doi.org/10.7861/clinmedicine.10-1-50.

Leader League (2020). "COVID-19 Success Stories: How Hong Kong Curbed the Spread of the Virus," accessed 26 March 2021, available at https://www.leadersleague.com/en/news/covid-19-success-stories-how-hong-kong-curbed-the-spread-of-the-virus.

Leung, G. M., Ho, L. M., Lam, T. H., and Hedley, A. J. (2009). "Epidemiology of SARS in the 2003 Hong Kong Epidemic," *Hong Kong Medical Journal*, 15 (Suppl. 9), 12–16.

Mainichi (2020). "Japan to Ban Resale of Masks at High Prices Amid Coronavirus-Triggered Shortage," accessed 26 March 2021, available at https://mainichi.jp/english/articles/20200306/p2a/00m/0na/007000c.

Mercer (2020). "Coronavirus Response Survey," accessed 27 July 2020, available at https://www.mercer.com.hk/our-thinking/healthy-people-healthy-business/prevailing-from-covid19.html.

Ming Pao (2020). "[Wuhan feiyan] Weisheng Shu Zhang Bei Zhiyi Yin Jin Meng Mian Fa Mei Huyu Dai Kouzhao Lin Zheng: Huaiyi Wo Du Zhong You Shaoshao Liyou (Wuhan Coronavirus: Department of Health Suspected of Not Calling for Mask-Wearing Due to Anti-Mask Law, Carrie Lam: It is Even More Reasonable to Doubt Me)," accessed 26 March 2021, available at https://news.mingpao.com/ins/%E6%B8%AF%E8%81%9E/article/20200125/s00001/1579948485293/.

Ming Pao Weekly (2020). "Gang Ren Zijiu 8 Kuan Bendi Kouzhao Luxu Touchan (Hong Kongers Save Themselves: Eight Types of Local Masks Gradually put into Production)," accessed 13 September 2021, available at https://www.mpweekly.com/culture/%E6%AD%A6%E6%BC%A2%E8%82%BA%E7%82%8E-%E6%96%B0%E5%9E%8B%E5%86%A0%E7%8B%80%E7%97%85%E6%AF%92-%E5%8F%A3%E7%BD%A9-139735.

Oriental Daily (2020). "Shimin Hong Zhengfu Tai Chi Tuixing Kouzhao Ling Fangyi Zhi Neng Kao Ziji (Citizens Blast Government for Making Mask-Wearing Mandatory Too Late; Can Only Fight the Virus by Ourselves)," accessed 13 September 2021, available at https://hk.on.cc/hk/bkn/cnt/news/20200722/bkn-20200722163151045-0722_00822_001.html.

Reuters (2020). "Hong Kongers Set Up Face Mask Factory Amid Coronavirus Panic Buying," accessed 26 March 2021, available at https://jp.reuters.com/article/china-health-hongkong-factory/hong-kongers-set-up-face-mask-factory-amid-coronavirus-panic-buying-idINKBN20F0VT.

Saiidi, Uptin (2020). "How Hong Kong Beat Coronavirus and Avoided Lockdown," *CNBC*, accessed 26 March 2021, available at https://www.cnbc.com/2020/07/03/how-hong-kong-beat-coronavirus-and-avoided-lockdown.html.

Wan, K. M., Ho, K. K., Wong, N., and Chiu, A. (2020). Fighting COVID-19 in Hong Kong: The effects of community and social mobilization. *World Development*, 134, 105055.

Worldometers (2021). "COVID-19 Coronavirus Pandemic," accessed 9 September 2021, available at https://www.worldometers.info/coronavirus/?utm_campaign=homeAdvegas1.

Xu, R. H., He, J. F., Evans, M. R., Peng, G. W., Field, H. E., Yu, D. W., Lee, C. K., Luo, H. M., Lin, W. S., Lin, P., Li, L. H., Liang, W. J., Lin, J. Y., and Schnur, A. (2004). Epidemiologic clues to SARS origin in China. *Emerging Infectious Diseases*, 10(6), 1030–1037.

https://doi.org/10.1142/9789811253737_0006

Chapter 6

Community Work and Social Support for Singaporeans during COVID-19

Wong Chong Wai, Kenneth, PBM

COVID-19 virus, which was reported to have originated from a local Chinese seafood and poultry market in Wuhan, China, has spread to at least 177 countries, afflicting more than 92.3 million people and at least 1.98 million people's lives have been taken away by the infection.[1] The figures are still on the rise with no sight of slowing down. Due to the alarming levels of proliferation and severity of infections (coupled with the alarming levels of inaction), World Health Organization (WHO) characterized this global widespread virus as a pandemic on 11 March 2020.

In the global proliferation, Singapore was not spared too. On 23 January 2020, Singapore registered its first imported case, a 66-year-old man from Wuhan and subsequently, on 4 February 2020, Singapore had its first case of infection in the community, a 28-year-old Singaporean who worked at Yong Thai Hang, a Chinese health products shop in Lavender which was popularly patronized by Chinese travelers. Since then, the Multi-Ministry Taskforce has been implementing several measures to curb the spread of the virus in the community, including setting

[1] World Health Organization (2020). "Coronavirus Disease (COVID-19) Situation Report — 192," accessed 31 July 2020, available at https://www.who.int/docs/default-source/coronaviruse/situation-reports/20200730-covid-19-sitrep-192.pdf?sfvrsn=5e52901f_4.

up a Multi-Agencies Contract Tracing Taskforce to trace possible individuals who might have been in contact with confirmed positive COVID-19 patients to carry out the necessary quarantine procedures. Building on this contact tracing effort, The Government Technology Agency (GovTech) developed a mobile application, TraceTogether, to assist in island-wide contact tracing. To better disseminate updates of COVID-19 situation in Singapore, a Short Message Service (SMS) system was launched for Singaporeans to subscribe to the updating services where Ministry of Health (MOH) can provide daily updates on the status of COVID-19 infections. Since then, public cautions were increased and communications were clearly communicated.

Though infected community cases were low, a crisis was building up quietly, unseen and unexpected by most in Singapore. With a population of about 5.7 million, the resident's population comprises approximately 4 million citizens/permanent residents and a non-resident's population of close to 1.6 million.[2] Yvette Tan from *BBC* reported that "Singapore is home to more than 300,000 low-wage foreign workers from countries like India and Bangladesh, who mainly work in industries like construction and manufacturing."[3] For these low-wage foreign workers, their employers have to provide accommodations at their own costs and, in order to save costs, many foreign workers' dormitories are overcrowded with cramped living conditions. As COVID-19 viruses can spread through exposure to respiratory droplets carrying infectious virus infection, some researches have shown that COVID-19 virus infections can occur from airborne exposure to the virus under certain circumstances, the living environment of these foreign workers appears to have unintended consequences of the virus spreading within the foreign workers' community.

Indeed, the spread of COVID-19 in the local foreign dormitories was unexpectedly rapid, causing an urgent case for swift action to be taken to isolate the affected workers and dormitories sites. At the national coordinating level, several locations were selected as Community Care Facility (CCF), such as D'Resort NTUC, Singapore Expo Convention Hall,

---

[2] Department of Statistics Singapore (2020). "Singapore Population," accessed 20 January 2021, available at https://www.singstat.gov.sg/modules/infographics/population.

[3] Yvette Tan (2020). "COVID-19 Singapore: A 'Pandemic of Inequality' Exposed," accessed 20 January 2021, available at https://www.bbc.com/news/world-asia-54082861#:~:text=Singapore%20is%20home%20to%20more,provide%20accommodation%2C%20at%20a%20cost.

Changi Exhibition Centre, to house COVID-19 patients who were clinically well but still test positive as well as newly confirmed cases with mild symptoms who do not require extensive treatment. This arrangement allows hospitals to free up their beds and medical facilities for patients who may be in more critical medical situation. In January 2021, Singapore recorded a total of 59,505 cases, with close to 54,508 cases coming from dormitory[4] (MOH, 2021). Though Singapore has such a high number of COVID-19 cases, it has a 99.5% of recovery rate (59,196 cases recovered) and 29 death cases.[5]

The number of infected cases in the dormitory as compared to the number of infected cases in the community show a stark difference between the two "communities." The outbreak of the COVID-19 in the foreign workers' dormitories sparked some debates on the neglected living conditions and welfare of these migrant workers — the sudden (media) interest and concern shown in the community, coupled with the new safety and hygiene regulations set out by the Ministry of Manpower and Ministry of Health, resulted in a surge of local-initiated charity drives and national efforts in curbing the community spread in Singapore. For instance, in dormitories where migrant workers were infected with COVID-19, facilities were deep-cleaned and personal belongings were discarded. Charitable organizations and individuals came together to organize donation drives to encourage people to donate their pre-loved items, such as clothing apparels, bags, shoes, toiletries, and many more, to donate to the affected migrant workers.

Many organizations also take on social media to show appreciation to the frontline workers and essential workers who are vital in maintaining essential services for Singapore's economy, healthcare, and security during this critical moment. Videos, letters, songs, were written and composed and dedicated to the frontline workers and essential workers. A #SGUnited social media movement was launched by Ministry of Culture, Community and Youth to rally fellow Singaporeans to show support and appreciation to other fellow Singaporeans and workers who have been affected by COVID-19.

---

[4] Ministry of Health (2021). "COVID-19 Situation Report," accessed 30 January 2021, available at https://covidsitrep.moh.gov.sg/ on 31 January 2021.

[5] Google News (2021). "Coronavirus (COVID-19). Singapore," accessed 3 February 2021, available at https://news.google.com/covid19/map?hl=en-SG&mid=%2Fm%2F06t2t&gl=SG&ceid=SG%3Aen.

For instance, home-grown singer and music composer, Dick Lee, rallied other singers such as Rahimah Rahim, Shabir, Taufik Batisah as well as Mediacorp artistes Desmond Tan, Felicia Chin, Rebecca Lim, and Vernetta Lopez to come together for the "Sing Together, Singapore!," biggest-ever sing-along event, to show appreciation to front-liners, migrant workers, and fellow Singaporeans who are coping with the 2-months Circuit Breaker (CB). The CB is a partial lockdown of Singapore where people are regulated to stay-at-home and is only allowed to travel out of house to perform essential duties, to uplift the emotional, physiological spirits of the people! These singers were backed by the 900 members of the Voices of Singapore choir. During the CB period, some healthcare workers were discriminated by fellow commuters in the fear that they may spread the COVID-19 virus to them and were consequently shunned by some private transport providers.

Grab Singapore, a Singapore-based technology company offering ride-hailing transport services, food delivery and payment solutions, launched the GrabCare transport hailing service for healthcare professionals to book a ride home from the National Centre for Infectious Diseases (NCID) and Tan Tock Seng Hospital (TTSH), two primary locations where COVID-19 patients can receive medical treatment. It was heartening to see that more than 2,000 drivers stepped forth and became part of the initiative to provide hailing transportation for the healthcare workers. Food & Beverage Restaurants such as McDonald, Pek Kio Market & Food Centre, Old Chang Kee, The Mix Bar, Kitchen Kumars, and many more, also chipped in to offer free food and drinks to healthcare workers who have been going above and beyond their call of duty amid the COVID-19 pandemic outbreak. Hotels too, also provided free hotel stays to healthcare workers to show appreciation for the selfless sacrifices. One good example was Pan Pacific Hotels Group which provided 25,000 nights of complimentary stays to staff from SingHealth, National Healthcare Group (NHG), and National University Health System (NUHS).[6]

COVID-19 took the world by surprise. Many countries were not prepared in dealing with the pandemic. Having experienced Severe Acute Respiratory Syndrome (SARS) in 2003, Singapore's healthcare system

---

[6] Mothership (2020). "Pan Pacific Hotels Offering 25,000 Free Stays to S'pore Healthcare Workers from Dec. 1, 2020–Mar. 31, 2021," accessed 2 February 2021, available at https://mothership.sg/2020/08/pan-pacific-free-stay-healthcare-workers/.

had drawn upon this experience to enhance its pandemic preparedness response. Although the emergence of COVID-19 has now put these preparations to the test, there are still areas which caught Singapore unprepared. One of the areas was the availability of masks for the population. As advised by WHO, to minimize the spread of the infection, it is recommended for everyone to wear face mask in public areas.

This caught Singapore off-guard. With the surge in the global demand of face masks and the raw materials, some earlier arrangements with overseas partners and manufacturers to produce surgical masks could not be realized, as countries imposed export controls on medical supplies. Since mid-February, Singapore has been thinking of different strategies to ramp up its domestic production of surgical masks to meet the needs of healthcare workers, including setting up local production plants in Singapore.

To ensure every citizens in Singapore have access to free masks, a huge mobilization exercise was called to conduct mask distribution exercise island-wide. This exercise mobilized Singapore's military personnel from the Singapore Armed Forces, staff from Temasek Foundation, Grassroots volunteers from The People's Association, to set up various distribution centers around Singapore to make collection of masks hassle-free for the people. While this was a national initiative, individuals and organizations also chipped in to provide reusable masks for the lesser-privileged group. One such initiatives was the Masks Sewn With Love — a community project to sew reusable cloth masks by the community (volunteers) for the community, and they were distributed to the vulnerable groups in shelter and homes, cleaners and domestic helpers; including vulnerable kids and their families within the respective estates.

While it may be a given for people to cope well at home during the CB, family and domestic violence was on the rise during the period.[7] Single elderly individuals who were immobilized may face difficulties getting relatives to run errands for them while other elderly Singaporeans may not be able to withstand boredom of being cooped at home. There is a Chinese saying "远亲不如近邻，远水救不了近火" which literally means "distant water cannot put out a nearby fire, and a distant relative is not as helpful as a close neighbor." With this mind-set and the mission to

[7] Jean Lau (2020). "More Cases of Family Violence during Circuit Breaker; Police to Proactively Help Victims," accessed 1 February 2021, available at https://www.straitstimes.com/singapore/courts-crime/coronavirus-more-cases-of-family-violence-during-circuit-breaker-police-to.

revive the *kampong* spirit, GoodHood.SG, a ground-up initiative, was set up to connect people who stay in close proximity to provide and receive help in an easier and convenient way. Residents can offer to help their fellow neighbors with items or services needed through the GoodHood.SG mobile app such as doing grocery runs for those under home-quarantine or offering items they may need and make a few new friends in the neighborhood in the hope of strengthening social connections within the neighborhood.

Not only the elderly were affected during the CB period, many students were also taken by surprise by the need to continue their learning through Home-Based Learning. However, financially challenged students may not have access to computers, internet connection or the basic conducive home environment to allow them to concentrate on their online learning. IT Company, Lenovo Singapore launched the "I Learn U Learn" initiative, donating laptops to financially challenged students from the Institute of Technical Education (ITE), to allow them to continue their Home-Based Learning without equipment worries. While doing so, Lenovo Singapore also encouraged students who have benefited from this initiative to pay back their dues in the form of volunteering their time and services back to the community.

Youth organizations such as the National Youth Achievement Award (NYAA) Council Singapore, called on students from Primary and Secondary schools to create videos and hashtag, #WeStandVidYou, to show appreciation to their teachers who have painstakingly taken the time and efforts to make Home-Based Learning interesting and to cater to the different learning needs of their students, just to make sure that their students are able to understand the lesson contents, as it was not an easy feat to change their lesson delivery mode from a classroom-based concept to online learning.

It is worth noting that that the spirit of giving to fellow Singaporeans was strong despite the COVID-19 pandemic which had affected many. In the first 5 months of 2020 alone, S$90 million was donated to the Community Chest, the Community Foundation of Singapore's Sayang Sayang Fund which was set up in February 2020, and to the online donation platform Giving.sg.[8] As the saying goes "Adversity brings out all the qualities in man." Through this episode, many organizations and

[8] Goh Yan Han (2020). "S'poreans Donated $90m in First Five Months of 2020, Equal to Whole of Last Year's Donations," accessed 1 February 2021, available at

individuals around Singapore have displayed their act of kindness and the spirit of "gotong royong" in various means and forms — donating and sewing masks for fellow Singaporeans and non-Singaporeans (e.g., foreign workers), distributing hand sanitizers, educating public (especially seniors) on knowing COVID-19 and how to protect oneself, helping neighbors who are serving home quarantine to buy food and groceries, providing free food and showing appreciation to our healthcare and frontline workers, volunteering as Safe Distancing Ambassadors and Swabbers, taking on social media to conduct recreational activities to keep each other occupied during the CB and many more. These are just some ground-up initiatives taken by fellow Singaporeans to lend a helping hand to those in need, on top of the various Government initiatives and financial supported which has been introduced through four different budgets — Unity, Resilience, Solidarity, and Fortitude, an unprecedented move in Singapore's history which amounts to almost S$100 billion, all funded through state revenues and reserves.

The global spread of COVID-19 has not only caused an unprecedented global health crisis but also impacted on the global economy — with major economies taking an inward-looking approach, shutting down their borders and trade supplies. Singapore, a country heavily dependent on international trade, was deeply affected by the economic downturn, causing various industries to shut down and companies taking a conservative approach to save costs — retrenching workers and even shutting down the business operations, raising the unemployment rate in Singapore to 2.4%, recording the highest jobless rate in 10 years.[9] To cushion the economic impacts and help Singapore workers cope with the financial hardship that they may face, several schemes have been introduced by the Singapore Government.

Among them were the Temporary Relief Fund and the COVID-19 Support Grant. Temporary Relief Fund provided a one-time financial assistance of S$500 while COVID-19 Support Grant provided monthly cash grant of S$800 for a period of 3 months. These two support schemes were set up to help Singapore residents deal with immediate short-term

---

https://www.straitstimes.com/singapore/singaporeans-donate-90million-in-first-five-months-of-2020-equal-to-whole-of-last-years on 1 February 2021.

[9] Ministry of Manpower (2020). "Labour Market Report First Quarter 2020," accessed 31 July 2020, available at https://www.mom.gov.sg/newsroom/press-releases/2020/0615-labour-market-report-first-quarter-2020.

financial challenges caused by retrenchment, who suffered substantial loss of personal income due to COVID-19, or placed on involuntary no-pay leave during this period. As the economy is far from recovering, more social support schemes were rolled out to provide further assistance to both Singapore workers and businesses. The Workfare Special Payment provided a total cash payout of S$3,000 for eligible low-wage Singaporean workers aged 35 and above for Work Years 2019 and 2020 while the Jobs Support Programme supported employers in selected sectors (e.g., aviation and built environment) in receiving wage support of 10–50% offset for the first S$4,600 of monthly wages paid to each local employee.[10]

The Courage Fund provided relief to vulnerable Singaporeans who are facing loss of income or struggling with additional caregiving duties and additional expenses for essential items while the Invictus Fund supports Social Service Agencies to continue delivering services to clients safely and effectively during COVID-19.[11] There are other forms of social support such as cash disbursement through Care and Support Scheme, grocery vouchers, additional GST Voucher — U-Save, grants to Self-Help Groups and Community Development Councils, and Service and Conservancy Charges Rebate.[12]

Singapore, being a cosmopolitan country, consists of a diverse workforce with expats from all over the world. Malaysia, Singapore's closest neighboring country, has thousands of Malaysians commuting between Singapore and Malaysia on a daily basis. With the announcement of CB which forced non-essential businesses from operating normally, coupled with the announcement by the Malaysian Government on the implementation of Movement Control Order (MCO), many Malaysians were caught in a dilemma as to whether they should stay in Singapore and continue to work or risk returning back to Malaysia to face uncertainties of when the COVID-19 pandemic situation will stabilize. They were also unsure of when they can return back to Singapore.

The announcements of CB and MCO by both Singaporean and Malaysian governments forced these workers to choose between returning

---

[10] Gov.sg (2020). "COVID-19 Support Schemes," accessed 1 February 2021, available at https://www.gov.sg/article/jobsgohere-covid-support.

[11] *Ibid.*

[12] Ministry of Finance (2020). "Budget 2020," accessed 1 February 2021, available at https://www.singaporebudget.gov.sg/budget_2020/budget-measures/care-and-support-package.

to Malaysia to be with their loved ones but possibly stay unemployed, or staying behind in Singapore without any housing or family support. Many of these Malaysian workers perform jobs that are critical to the functioning of Singapore's economy. Malaysians who chose to stay behind in Singapore are facing challenges in finding affordable accommodations. In view of this, Better.SG was launched to mobilize Singaporeans to help Malaysian workers in Singapore during this difficult time and possibly rally some Singaporeans to offer their extra rooms to the Malaysian workers to tide them through this crisis. A local initiative, Ops Roof Up, was put together by a group of "can do" Singaporeans to provide sleeping bags and basic toiletries for stranded Malaysians who were affected by the sudden announcement of the MCO by the Malaysian Government. Singapore's Ministry of Social and Family Development was also called upon to provide temporary relief shelter for workers who are affected by the sudden announcement. Besides providing temporary shelter to those in need, corporations, big and small, came forth to provide employment opportunities to people who were retrenched.

Through the SGUnited Traineeship program initiated by the government to rally corporations to collectively provide more than 21,000 traineeship positions, students who recently graduated or are near graduation can then apply for these job opening. This initiative aims to help these graduates find relevant job employment opportunities and further develop their industry-relevant skills, notwithstanding the current global economic atmosphere, to boost their employability in preparation for eventual economic recovery.

At the local level, several Members of Parliament are using their own network to rally more corporations to come on board to offer job employment opportunities. One such example is the Jobs Connect @ Joo Chiat, a local initiative mooted by the Minister of Culture, Community and Youth and Second Minister for Law, Mr. Edwin Tong, who is also the Member of Parliament for Marine Parade GRC (Joo Chiat). The Taskforce garner support from businesses operating in the Joo Chiat area to offer employment opportunities to the local residents. So far, more than 100 job employment opportunities were generated for the local residents. To provide further assistance to affected residents, Corporations and Foundations, such as Ngee Ann Kongsi (NAK), Apricot Capital Foundation, Business China, just to name a few, are collaborating with Community Development Councils (CDCs) to set up COVID-19 Relief Fund to provide financial assistance to the residents in the form of utilities vouchers, grocery vouchers, cash disbursement, professional workshops, and program to support businesses and residents.

Combating against COVID-19 pandemic is a long battle fight. Even as Singapore was hailed as having the "gold standard" due to the government's strong handling of the pandemic outbreak through contract tracing, medical support and the way her citizens responded to the community outbreak, there is room for constant improvements as well, such as coping mechanisms for the community spread in the foreign workers' dormitories. From CB to Phase 2 and now moving into Phase 3, the spread of COVID-19 virus in the community and dormitories have come under control, with majority of the infected cases imported. The daily news coverage, Whatsapps, and social media updates from MOH kept citizens updated with the latest development of the COVID-19 pandemic status in Singapore. This, has become the formal channel of getting authenticated information, debunking any possible fabrications or fake news contents. In order to keep the population safe from COVID-19, other than taking all the safety measures such as refraining from touching public objects, maintaining safe distancing, wearing face masks, getting the population vaccinated is probably the best way forward in pandemic mitigation measures.

Knowing the importance of having access to the vaccines, the Singapore Government took the "gamble" and invested in some pharmaceutical companies at the very initial stage of the vaccine development. The "gamble" yielded positive returns with Pfizer-BioNTech COVID-19 vaccine becoming the first vaccine worldwide to be approved by the British Government and Singapore became the first nation in Asia to receive doses of the Pfizer-BioNTech COVID-19 vaccine on 21 December 2020, thanks to a coordinated approach between the Government, the scientific community, and industry partners.

Prior to the arrival of the Pfizer-BioNTech COVID-19 vaccine, planning was already underway to prioritize the groups of Singaporean receiving the vaccines first. Healthcare and frontline workers will be given the priority to receive the vaccination. Singaporean leaders, including the Prime Minister of Singapore and several Cabinet Ministers, also took the vaccines to give the public the confidence in showing that the vaccine is safe and everyone should go ahead to take the vaccine when the opportunity becomes available.

To encourage the whole population to be vaccinated, vaccination cost is fully borne by the government. At the community level, seniors aged

70 years old and above, residing in Tanjong Pagar and Ang Mo Kio divisions were the first batch to receive their first doses of vaccines. Vaccinations will be progressively rolled out to seniors across the Singapore island from mid-February 2021 onward. It is projected that, by end March 2021, all 24 Housing Development Board (HDB) towns will be equipped with vaccination centers, making the vaccination convenient and easily accessible to all and everyone (including non-citizens like migrant workers). So far, 113,000 people have been vaccinated[13] and the People's Association is mobilizing its grassroots leaders to attend briefings and trainings to conduct house visits to encourage people to get vaccinated.

Leading the battle against COVID-19, Singapore government and various stakeholders in the community, through the Public, Private and People approach, rallied together to address the various social, health, financial challenges that arose in the pandemic. The battle against COVID-19 pandemic is far from over and Singapore, as well as countries around the world, should never let their guard down. Many countries including Hong Kong, Australia, and Western countries are facing several waves of outbreaks, forcing the countries to go into partial/full lockdown once again, affecting their economies.

[13] Ministry of Health (2021). "Update on COVID-19 Vaccination Programme: 28 January 2021," accessed 2 February 2021, available at https://www.moh.gov.sg/news-highlights/details/update-on-covid-19-vaccination-programme.

Part 3

COVID-19 and Science

https://doi.org/10.1142/9789811253737_0007

Chapter 7

COVID-19 and Iran: Investigating the Interconnection of Modern Science and Islam

Satoshi Abe

Introduction

Statistically, Iran is one of the countries in the Middle East that has been most severely affected by COVID-19, at the time of writing in October 2021. The country's known cases of infection thus far total 5.8 million, the second highest count after Turkey, while the number of COVID-19–related deaths is reported to have reached 125,000, the highest in the region.[1] This writing reviews and provides in-depth accounts of the unfolding of the COVID-19 pandemic in Iran, from its early phase when the country detected the first cases of infection in February 2020 to the present when the virus continues to grimly affect the everyday lives of its people. This chapter calls to attention Iran's distinctive sociocultural background and historical conditions against which the pandemic takes its course. In particular, it looks at religious dimensions of the pandemic in the country, as Islam serves as the state religion that guides various state programs, including those of COVID-19 public health measures.

[1] All the statistical data shown in this chapter comes from the Reuters COVID-19 tracker, available at https://graphics.reuters.com/world-coronavirus-tracker-and-maps/countries-and-territories/iran/.

Religious debates about COVID-19 have generated a wide spectrum of Islamic viewpoints through which the crises of the pandemic are addressed and problematized, thus amplifying the religious frames of reference through which the pandemic is understood in the country. Given the historical and cultural significance of Islam in Iran,[2] the discussions of public health management by the government are neither reducible to nor explicable by science alone. What religious perspectives and measures have emerged in Iran in a field that is predominantly conceptualized by scientific reasoning and scientific findings? In what ways are agreements and disagreements concerning public health measures addressed and debated among its religious leaders? What is the nature of the contention regarding the status of modern science among them? These are the questions this chapter seeks to address.

COVID-19 and Iran: A Timeline

Iran confirmed its first cases of both COVID-19 infection and death on 19 February 2020. They traced the very first evidence of this mysterious disease to an ancient, mid-sized religious city called Qom. Qom is located about 85 miles southwest of the country's capital, Tehran, and is known to be a religious home for Shi'i Muslims, where Fatemeh, a sister of the eighth Shi'i Imam, is enshrined. The city attracts millions of pilgrims every year from both inside and outside Iran. In the beginning of the pandemic, many leaders, from government officials to religious clerics, downplayed and dismissed the cases of COVID-19 as the West's plots, perhaps as intentional obstruction of the then-upcoming parliamentary elections. As the infection and death counts continued to grow and showed no sign of declining, however, they were eventually forced to take action against the spread of the virus. The Ministry of Health and Medical Education (henceforth the "Ministry of Health") came to the forefront and began to lead the nationwide efforts to contain the virus by, for example, publicizing the statistics about COVID-19 and issuing preventive measures and public health guidelines for holding social events.

Despite such government efforts to combat the disease, Iran experienced the first wave of the virus in late March 2020, and the government

[2] See, for example, Haider (2014), Keddie (2006), and Mottahedeh (1985) on the historical and cultural significance of Islam in Iran.

decided to restrict some public activities and the use of public facilities. The government ordered schools, mosques, bazaars (except for the shops supplying necessities), and shopping centers across the country to shut for the 15-day Persian new year holiday, *nourūz*.[3] At the same time, due to the highly constrained financial situation prompted by US-led sanctions, they asked the International Monetary Fund for 5 billion US dollars in emergency funds to fight the outbreak, a move that had never been undertaken since the Islamic Revolution in 1979.[4] These systematic approaches by the government temporarily helped slow down the transmission of the virus and cleared the way to authorize less restrictive measures in public. Yet, this phase turned out to be the beginning of another wave to come in May 2020.

Witnessing the already crippled economy further deteriorating with the surge of COVID-19, the Rouhani administration shifted their mitigation strategy, this time allowing business activities to operate with reduced working hours, to allow some economic activity while at the same time attempting to keep movements of people at bay. The authorities in the country, for example, required citizens who used public transportation to wear masks and strictly enforced lockdowns and night-time curfews in those areas with a high risk of infection.[5] To put it succinctly, balancing the economy and public health became a key point of debate among policymakers in the administration. This strategy of allowing for business activities in tandem with public health restrictions — or their easing — has become their main approach to withstand the outbreak. Against this background, government officials discuss and make decisions about whether mass gathering events should be allowed. For example, after many rounds of discussions, the administration decided to carry out the national college entrance exam called *konkūr* and the annual religious ceremonies in August 2020 on the condition that public health protocols be strictly observed. Furthermore, secondary schools that had been closed for half a year by that time were allowed to reopen in early September 2020.

[3] https://www.bbc.com/persian/iran-51768535.

[4] https://www.wsj.com/articles/u-s-to-block-irans-request-to-imf-for-5-billion-loan-to-fight-coronavirus-11586301732.

[5] https://www.ilna.news/بخش-اجتماعی-10821605/ممنوعیت-تردد-بین-استانی-از-ساعت-سه-شنبه-خرداد-تا-ساعت-دوشنبه-خرداد; https://www.irna.ir/news/83819714/استفاده-از-ماسک-در-اتوبوس-های-تهران-اجباری-است.

It was around this time, however, that cases of infection began surging again and that the alert level was raised to the highest, coded red, in almost all parts of the country.[6] This alarming situation resulted in the enforcement of more strict regulations, especially in big cities where cases of COVID-19 infection and death were disproportionately concentrated; these regulations included the temporary closure of educational institutions and shopping centers, tightening of traffic controls between cities, mask-wearing mandates in public, and imposition of fines against protocol violators. These tighter restrictions proved to be insufficient to prevent another wave from ravaging the country, however. The cumulative cases of infections quickly surpassed the landmark count of 1 million by early December of 2020.

In their continuing fight against the pandemic, Iran, amid the third wave, managed to strike a deal with Russia for the Russian-manufactured vaccine "Sputnik V" and started vaccination programs in February 2021 that prioritized healthcare workers and elders. Their decision to receive the Russian vaccine, despite their peculiar historical relations with Russia, deeply reflects international politics and the geopolitical alignment in which Iran is currently situated. Ayatollah Khamenei, the Supreme Leader, repeatedly expresses his distrust of any political gestures toward Iran by the US and Europe and judged any vaccines traceable to them to be "not trustworthy," decisively ruling out the possibility of importing these vaccines to the country.[7] Instead, Iran turned to Russia, China, and India, as well as Cuba with whom they jointly operate vaccine programs, for the procurement and production of COVID-19 vaccines. A downward trend of cases occurred around the time the vaccination program began.

The two-week celebration of the Persian New Year, which started in late March 2021, another major nationwide event in Iran that involves the movement of people across the country, upended the downward trend of infection cases. It significantly contributed to the rise of the fourth wave of the pandemic in Iran. Health officials decided to allow citizens to travel in less affected areas across the country, which subsequently opened the floodgate for the widespread movement of travelers. According to a newspaper report, the amount of road travel increased 100 fold compared with

[6] https://www.irna.ir/news/84071544/بیستم-مهر-ماه-با-مهمترین-اخبار-کرونا-در-استان-ها.

[7] https://www.isna.ir/news/99101914261/رهبر-معظم-انقلاب-ورود-واکسن-آمریکایی-و-انگلیسی-به-کشور-ممنوع.

the previous year when travel was kept to a minimum amid the growing sense of urgency toward reducing infection risk.[8]

With the fourth wave underway, restriction orders were put back in place; for example, only essential services sectors were allowed to operate, while dine-in restaurants, cinemas, and shopping centers were ordered to stop and shut down. Yet, many Iranians began to show signs of fatigue over repeating COVID-19 restrictions and reportedly stopped following public health protocols, an indication that strategies that heavily rely on restrictions are not enough to contain the outbreak. President Rouhani expressed his frustration in a press conference in April 2021 that only 56% of Iran's people were following public health guidelines issued by the Ministry of Health and pleaded that they become more considerate about the preventive measures that require mutual commitments.[9]

Before the fourth wave faded entirely, Iran began to experience the fifth wave in June 2021, this time with much greater intensity and severity compared to previous waves. As the Delta variant quickly became dominant and rampant throughout the country, the virus brought deadly consequences to Iran with the highest count yet in terms of daily cases of infection and death. Although vaccination programs had started in February 2021, their progress has been rather slow; after 8 months, about 47% of the total population had received 2 doses of COVID-19 vaccine at the time of writing in late October of 2021.

Public Health Guidelines Issued by the Ministry of Health

Throughout the entire period of the pandemic, modern science has provided a conceptual framework to identify, problematize, and combat the virus in Iran. The Ministry of Health is orchestrating the preventive measures and programs nationwide based on scientific schemes. With the eruption of the COVID-19 pandemic, the field of public health has increasingly become an object of scientific research, particularly

[8] https://www.irna.ir/news/84282117/بیماران-کرونا-که-به-سفر-رفتند-جریمه-می-شوند.

[9] https://www.farsnews.ir/news/14000121000124/روحانی-اولین-علت-موج-چهارم-کرونا-ورود-ویروس-انگلیسی-از-کشور-عراق-بوده.

concerning the technical management of the virus.[10] This section demonstrates some distinctive ways in which public health is managed in Iran based on scientific understandings of virus transmission; it looks at the Ministry of Health's safety protocol manual written for exam administrators and color-coded-maps as examples.[11]

The Ministry of Health's safety manual provides up-to-date information about virus transmission, its key characteristics, and precautionary measures to be reviewed before administering exams. Its contents cover a wide range of subject matter, such as virus-infection protection, food operations, and ventilation in the building under the section entitled "actions to control a healthy work environment (*eqdāmāt-e kontrolī salāmat-e moḥīṭ va kār*)." The conceptual schemes provided in the protocol are based on a scientific understanding of public health. The foreword of the manual captures this scientific way of thinking pointedly:

> Becoming aware of disease transmission is very important to control the disease. The mechanism of this virus's transmission is still not entirely clear, but, according to the latest information, the transmission of respiratory viruses from human to human occurs through coughing, sneezing, and discharge of secretions of the nose and mouth in a particular environment. (The Ministry of Health and Medical Education, 2021, p. 2)

For further introduction to the disease, it provides some examples of virus carriers in everyday objects, such as stair railings, electronic keypads, paper money, and office documents that would necessitate hand-touching of (contaminated) surfaces. These opening statements indicate that the virus is an object identifiable through scientific inquiries and that the control of its dissemination is the prime concern among the parties involved.

Precautionary measures in the manual are highly technical and makes no mention of the religious faith throughout the text. For example, the Ministry of Health repeatedly draws attention to the minimal distance between people of 1.5–1.8 meters — the scientifically proven distance

[10] See Daston (2000) and Pickering (1992) for critically studying the roles science plays in making the so-called scientific objects.

[11] The Ministry of Health archives and makes available for the public official health protocols they have issued for COVID-19. Available at https://behdasht.gov.ir/step2corona.

that the virus can travel and transmit in human interactions — when they speak about social distancing; test-takers, explains the manual, are required to be at least 1.5–1.8 meters from one another when entering or leaving the room,[12] administrators should keep 1.5–1.8 meters from test-takers when they take questions from them.[13] To illustrate another technical aspect of the protocol, in a section called "attention to vulnerable groups," the manual enumerates typical features seen in those individuals more susceptible to COVID-19 as follows: those with heart disease, high blood pressure, diabetes, respiratory-related diseases, or BMI (Body Mass Index) greater than 40.[14] In another instance, the administrators are instructed to host exams at maximum 20% capacity of the room and with windows open at 45 degrees.[15] The rooms selected must be at least 12 meters square and be equipped with proper ventilation systems.[16] Additionally, two doors in the room must be opened and arranged in such a way that the polluted air flows to the outside.[17] The manual concludes with detailed descriptions and illustrations on ways to wear personal protective gear (i.e., face shields, eye protection googles, gloves, and gowns) and ways to dispose them safely, stating that protective gear are essential tools to protect oneself from virus infection.[18] These precautionary measures exhibit some concrete examples of how scientific schemes are fashioned and incorporated into the field of public health by the Ministry of Health. They also indicate a critical role and status attributed to modern science in Iran.

The Iranian government relies on another scientifically-driven strategy to fight the COVID-19 pandemic. The Ministry of Health collects and closely tracks the cases of infections and deaths related to the disease. They compile and update those data on a daily basis and turn them into a color-coded map in which severely affected provinces are visibly differentiated from less severely affected ones. The colors of red, orange, yellow, and blue used in this map indicate the degree of infection incidence

---

[12] The Ministry of Health and Medical Education, 2021, p. 2.

[13] *Ibid.*, p. 11.

[14] *Ibid.*, p. 5.

[15] *Ibid.*, p. 8.

[16] *Ibid.*

[17] *Ibid.*

[18] *Ibid.*, pp. 17–22.

in that order, with red being the highest and blue being the lowest.[19] Moreover, the Ministry of Health determines official health guidelines that correspond with the classification of these colors. The guidelines are intended to help them oversee and regulate activities in differing realms of society, namely "administrative offices (*edārāt*)," "trades, bazaar, and services (*tejārī, bāzargānī va khādamātī*)," "education (*āmūzeshī*)," "culture and society (*farhangī va ejtemā'ī*)," and "traffic (*taraddodhā*)." The more severely the areas are affected by COVID-19 infections, the more restricted activities become. For the cities color-coded as blue, for example, all administrative workers can work in their respective offices, and they are allowed to have meetings in a closed room setting with the presence of 50 people at maximum. In red areas, however, more restrictions are put in place; administrative officers in essential services sectors need to limit their number in the workplace to a half, and the presence of office staff needs to be reduced to two-thirds. In addition, the number of meeting attendees is limited to 15 individuals maximum.

Similarly, this difference in degree of restriction is also evident in the realm of traffic flow. In blue areas, a nocturnal curfew will be effective between 9 p.m. and 3 a.m. In red areas, in addition to this nocturnal curfew, private vehicles with number plates from red areas are not allowed to enter any other cities. In parallel, private vehicles with number plates from non-red areas cannot enter any red cities. Although the concrete measures in the document have been updated over time depending on the course of COVID-19 in Iran, this systematic approach based on scientific data-collection remains the same. The Ministry of Health, with the support of the Islamic establishment, continues to base their decisions on science and employs it on the frontlines against the disease.

Religious Dimensions of the Pandemic

The fact that the first cases of COVID-19 infection and death occurred in the holy city of Qom surprised and dismayed some of the faithful for whom Qom, due to its divine status, should have been protected from disastrous incidents like this. Some objected to the government's decision

[19] Red areas represent those in which more than 10 people per 100,000 test positive for COVID-19, using the PCR test. The areas of orange, yellow, and blue denote those in which 6, 4, and 2 individuals per 100,000, respectively, test positive.

to close the holy Ma'sumeh mosque in Qom. A man publicly licked gates to demonstrate that the virus was not a threat and claimed that others could follow him and visit the holy shrine.[20] Groups of individuals similarly protested against the government's decision by crowding around the mosque gates to demand to pray inside and by turning to techniques prescribed by Islamic medicine to contend that Islam can be a legitimate curative guide for the containment of COVID-19. As these reactions unfolded, a variety of media sources (newspapers, online news, and social networking sites) captured and reported heated debates among both government officials and religious leaders as to how to most effectively contain the disease. Some religious leaders have issued statements about the pandemic from religious points of view and have given practical religious guidance on ways to confront the disease. This section highlights how they view their roles in the fight against COVID-19 and looks at how they incorporate science-based public health protocols into their agenda in their efforts to work alongside the government.

In their discussions on health issues, many religious scholars in Iran view health conditions as primarily being affected by two major components: those of the body (*badānīyat*) and those of the spirit (*ma'navīyat*).[21] They understand the former to be subject to the fields of medical doctors and public health specialists whom they generally refer to as *kārshenāsān or motakhassesān*. It is in the latter realm that the religious leaders exercise their expertise on interpretation of the Quran and the Hadith (words and deeds of the Prophet Mohammad). These texts generally serve as the foundational sources of reference through which they explain the events of the pandemic. They also provide the faithful with the religiously grounded views on and guidelines for preventive measures against COVID-19 that are distinct from those issued by the Ministry of Health. The existence of the seemingly demarcated domains of science and Islam does not, however, lead to the refutation of one domain over the other in the field of public health.[22] Rather, the handling of the pandemic by the

---

[20] https://aftabnews.ir/fa/news/641990/توقف-حضور-زائران-در-حرم%E2%80%8Cهای-مطهر-کشور-بخاطر-جلوگیری-از-شیوع-کرونا.

[21] https://www.hawzahnews.com/news/888926/برای-مقابله-با-بیماری-ها-باید-توأمان-به-اسباب-مادی-و-معنوی-توجه. See also Rahman (1980) to explore how humans are defined within the Islamic cosmology.

[22] This argument is applicable to emerging "scientific" fields in Iran, such as the environment (Abe, 2016, 2021), psychiatry (Behrouzan, 2016), and sexuality (Najmabadi, 2014).

religious leaders shows their general understanding that both domains are interrelated with each other and mutually contribute to improving health conditions. According to their views, care for both the body and the spirit, with specialized care by medical doctors and religious leaders respectively, is crucial for anyone to remain healthy during the pandemic.

In fact, many religious leaders turn to the Ministry of Health regarding the matter of bodily health and consistently urge to faithfully comply with the Ministry's public health protocols issued on numerous occasions. Their urgent requests to observe the public health protocols for major religious events is such an example. The Iranian government decided to permit its people to hold an annual mourning event on the ninth and tenth of *Muharram* in August 2020 to commemorate the death of the third Shi'i Imam, Imam Hossein.[23] A series of mourning rituals, such as weeping and chest-beating, normally proceeds with mass gatherings and movements in close contact. Given these aspects of the event, after the rounds of discussions at the national level, the Ministry of Health together with a religious association released a joint statement concerning public health protocols for *Muharram* ceremonies; the protocols touched on the technical aspects of event arrangement and coordination, especially on physical distance among participants, protective gear (i.e., masks), and detailed instructions about ritual proceedings.[24] The joint statement reveals and reflects some important ways in which religious leaders comprehend and approach pandemic-related health problems. It shows that these leaders favorably acknowledge the scientific schemes of public health as a way to combat the virus and thus see no conceptual contradiction or conflict between them and Islamic perspectives.

Similarly, at the time of fasting (*ramazān*) in June 2021, the Ministry of Health announced a health advisory to the entire nation with the intention of discouraging close contact at the gatherings that normally follow the sunset prayer.[25] During *ramazān*, Muslims are accustomed to gathering with family members and friends and to sharing fast-breaking meals upon the call to prayer for the sunset prayer. Such gatherings can easily trigger the spread of the virus. For this reason, Iran's Supreme Leader,

---

[23] https://www.irna.ir/news/83900849/پیچیده-ترین-پروژه-دوران-کرونا-در-ماه-محرم-اجرا-می-شود.

[24] *Ibid.*

[25] https://www.mehrnews.com/news/5187322/شب-های-قدر-مراسم-شرایط-رمضان-ماه-بهداشتی-های; https://behdasht.gov.ir/رعایت-پروتکل-های-بهداشتی-در-مراسم-های-ماه-مبارک-رمضان/خصوص-پروتکل-های-مرتبط-با-مراسم-های-ماه-مبارک-رمضان; اخبار/نامه-وزیر-بهداشت-در.

Ayatollah Khamenei, also issued a *fatvā* (a legal opinion by religious scholars) concerning the obligation of fasting during the COVID-19 pandemic and acknowledged the roles medical experts play in clarifying the decision to observe fasting or not.[26] This shows that religious leaders judge the Ministry of Health and their public health approach to be appropriate and necessary in curtailing the disease, and thereby frame that approach within their larger conceptual scheme that attends both to the body and the spirit. These handlings of social events during *ramazān* by the Ministry of Health and Ayatollah Khamenei demonstrate how the scientific schemes are incorporated into Islamic traditions in Iran.

Activities of Religious Leaders and Religious Debates

In addition to working alongside the Ministry of Health, religious leaders engage in a variety of activities to alleviate the stress experienced by the faithful due to the pandemic. What religious perspectives on the pandemic have emerged as a result of their relief activities? In what ways do they understand and deal with the changes brought about by the pandemic on religious rituals in which they conventionally play a vital role? These are the kinds of questions found in this section.

As the concerns over the disease proliferaton rapidly grew in the early phase, religious leaders began to speak about health measures that are grounded in Islamic concepts; these measures complement, yet differ in nature from the ones issued by the Ministry of Health. The religious leaders, assuming the validity of the dichotomy of the body and the spirit, addressed ways of strengthening the latter to counter the challenges posed by COVID-19. A variety of media outlets associated with seminary schools, most notably *Howzahnews*, reported such views online to their audience, who had stayed at home.

In these reports, the following three concepts have been presented as key practices to withstand the lingering outbreak: *do'ā*, *tavakkol*, and *tavassol*. *Do'ā* refers to supplicatory prayers performed at the end of the formal ritual prayers, by which guidance and protection are requested from God (Esposito, 2004, p. 70). It is a way to embody one's faith in God

[26] https://www.irna.ir/news/84290489/حکم-رهبر-انقلاب-درباره-روزه-ماه-رمضان-در-زمان-شیوع-کرونا.

and serves as a particular way to (re)connect with God in the Islamic faith.[27] *Do'ā*, a religious leader argues, becomes of critical importance for the faithful at a time when faith can be easily swayed by unexpected, disastrous incidents like the COVID-19 pandemic.[28]

Tavakkol, trust in God, refers to the practice of complete self-abandonment and one's total reliance on God, who is to provide for one's daily needs (Esposito, 2004, p. 316). *Tavassol* denotes the act of requesting divine assistance from a spiritual intermediary in times of difficulty (Esposito, 2004, pp. 138–139). Each of these practices is viewed as an essential aspect of the Islamic faith that facilitates one's ties with God and thereby helps reaffirm one's faith. In an interview, Hojjat al-Islam Mohammadi Abbasi Aghavi explains the interrelation of the first two concepts in the following manner: becoming adept at *tavakkol* means to become better at reading one's own desires through God in the act of *do'ā* and *do'ā* greatly facilitates one's understanding of God, which itself helps enhance humans' *tavakkol*.[29] In his reading, these practices are interrelated with each other and are, at the same time, discrete venues to reflect on and deepen one's faith. In a similar vein, religious leaders stress the importance to the successors of the Prophet of practicing *tavassol*, often as a way to enhance one's spirituality in confronting faith quandaries sparked by the pandemic.[30]

Funerals are another unique occasion in which religious leaders play a vital role and discussions concerning the correct forms of Islam are increasingly taking place due to the changes brought about by the pandemic. Because the occurrence of death has religious implications in Iran, religious leaders constitute an indispensable part in funeral processions. Upon the arrival at a mosque of the deceased's body wrapped in a white burial cloth, religious leaders recite Quranic verses and lead the prayers for the family of the deceased, an act intended to prepare the body for the Final Judgement.

---

[27] Haeri (2021) elaborates on the multi-layered dimensions of *do'ā* among religious practitioners in Iran.

[28] https://www.hawzahnews.com/news/891128/مهارت-توکل-به-خداوند-حال-روحی-و-جسمی-ما-را-بهبود-می-بخشد.

[29] *Ibid*.

[30] http://https://www.hawzahnews.com/news/888934/توجه-به-معنویات-در-کنار-رعایت-مسایل-بهداشتی-لازمه-غلبه-بر-کرونا.

After the funeral service, the family members transport the body to a burial site in a silent procession and normally bury it within 24 hours of his/her death. Thus, in Iran, funerals are a religiously driven, strictly scripted ritual that accompanies duly elaborate procedures. With the rapid surge in deaths due to the virus outbreak, more religious leaders have been called upon to fulfill their duties at funeral processions. Yet, the virus transmission that can occur from dead bodies to the living posed considerable challenges to a crucial aspect of the funeral: washing the deceased's body. A family member of the same gender as the deceased usually washes the body with water and soap before taking it to a mosque. Burying the dead in accordance with religious rituals is of extreme importance for Iranians who view the burial procession as a special way to pay homage to the deceased and as a representation of the solemn gateway for the deceased for the Judgment Day.

Against this background, not being able to wash the body for the funeral procession is such a serious matter in Iran (Bayatrizi *et al.*, 2021) that it prompted religious debates as to how the dead body ought to be treated (i.e., purified) under the exceptional circumstances of the COVID-19 outbreak. Two positions, although not far apart from each other, emerged on this issue. A group of religious scholars, on the one hand, argues that the dead body should not be washed during the pandemic due to the danger of virus transmission. Ayatollah Sane'i, for example, mentions that, if there exists a possibility of infection, one could refrain from conducting water purification on the dead body.[31] Other religious leaders like Ayatollah Khamenei and Ayatollah Zanjani declared otherwise; in consideration of international health protocols, they stated, the family of the deceased can proceed with ritual washing with another Islamic custom called *tayammom*.[32] *Tayammom* is the Islamic ritual of dry purification with sand, instead of water, and is performed in place of body washing, when no clean water is readily available.

Concerning the ritual washing performed on deceased bodies, the Iranian government adopted the calls of Ayatollah Khamenei and allowed its people to practice the ritual with health protocols implemented.[33] Regardless of the positions debated among the religious leaders, their reliance on scientific health protocols is evident and suggests that scientific

[31] https://www.bbc.com/persian/iran-features-51708527.

[32] *Ibid.*

[33] https://www.isna.ir/print/99013118259/قربانیان-کرونا-چگونه-دفن-می-شوند.

criteria provide a foundation for public health measures and are assimilated into Islamic traditions by religious leaders. In fact, the government instructed the house of ritual washing (*ghassāl-khāne*) to operate based on the Ministry of Health's health guidelines; to prevent virus transmission, they requested that any water used in the house not be drained out.[34] It is against this background of Islamic tradition buttressed by scientific understandings and findings that Islamic scholars began to adapt funerals that evolved from a physical onsite to a virtual format.

The danger of virus infection revealed through scientific studies impacted on the procedures of funerals themselves in Iran. Virtual funerals are becoming a more common option amid the outbreak and are beginning to replace a conventional face-to-face funeral that Iranians prefer for gatherings of families and relatives. Many companies found business opportunities in virtual funerals and now offer a variety of service plans that attend to individual needs and purposes with price options. For example, some companies prepare three types of funeral services: "economy," "religious special," and "gnostic special." The latter two types emphasize on Islamic features and include a ritual called the ceremony of mercy that makes the funeral more religious in nature. The first type offers only basic (and minimal) services and does not cover such extra assistances as electronic file edits and close-up photography that are available for the latter two. One organization advertised on their website the kinds of services readily available for online funerals. A long list includes: arrangement of the place (either the house of the deceased or a studio), time, and date; the circulation of ads on social networking sites and guest invitations; the creation of an event link for livestreaming; a poster, a banner, a condolence stand, and a charitable wreath; and memorial video clips and films.[35] Such online funerals became a feasible option not just among ordinary citizens but also among publicly well-known figures in Iran. Online news media, for example, reported virtual funerals held for a football star who had died of COVID-19 and a deceased religious cleric who previously worked for a governmental office.[36] A series of online funerals advertised and reported in the media provide insights into scientific

[34] *Ibid.*

[35] https://hejrantarhim.com/ختم-مجازی/?v=d6392e39ad2a.

[36] https://www.hawzahnews.com/news/929615/-مجازی-مرحوم-حجت-الاسلام-راستگو-برگزار-می-شود; https://www.ilna.news/بخش-ورزشی-7/1035753-برگزاری-مراسم-ختم-مجازی-برای-علی-انصاریان-از-طرف-باشگاه-پرسپولیس/مراسم-بزرگداشت.

findings about the virus transmission and their crucial changes to the format of funerals in Iran that are deeply rooted in Islamic traditions. Furthermore, they revealed that religious leaders generally show no sign of objections to these changes, and they incorporate scientific knowledge in such a way that Islamic rituals remain relevant and meaningful for the faithful during the pandemic. This does not, however, mean that no tensions or unanimous consent exist among religious leaders in Iran with regard to scientific measures taken against the virus, as seen in the next section.

Controversies about the Scientific Approach to COVID-19

One of the controversial figures who emerged in the Islamic community during the pandemic is a self-proclaimed Ayatollah, Abbas Tabrizian, who was allegedly trained in the principles of jurisprudence and Islamic medicine in Qom. Born in Najaf, Iraq, in 1343 (1964) and residing in Qom and Mashhad since the age of 18, he reportedly practiced Islamic medicine and have treated 150 patients with incurable diseases on a daily basis. He views modern medicine as too reliant on chemicals in treatments and has been highly critical of the intellectual foundation of science upon which it has been developed. A symbolic move intended to show his disdain for and mistrust of modern medicine came to the fore in January 2020, just before the virus hit Iran the following month. He posted a video clip in which he burned *Harrison's Principles of Internal Medicine*, purported to be an authoritative reference book of internal medicine in the international community.[37] Upon learning about this incident, the government ordered Tabrizian to close his office in Qom and leave the city.[38]

This incident prompted reactions from religious leaders and triggered religious debates concerning the credentials and status of modern science within Islamic intellectual traditions. Numerous leaders criticized Tabrizian's book-burning act, claiming that the act denotes his unilateral refutation of intellectual inquiry, scientific inquiry, and is uncharacteristic of their own intellectual establishment. As an example, Ayatollah Arafi,

[37] https://www.hawzahnews.com/news/883034/فیلم-آتشی-که-واکنش-حوزه-را-در-پی-داشت.

[38] https://www.irna.ir/news/83692826/ادعای-تازه-مدعی-طب-سنتی-کرونا-انتقام-خدا-از-اذیت-کنندگان-من.

head of Iran's seminary, in response to this incident issued a statement that the organization he represents values modern science, its way of inquiry, and scholarly critiques that might arise, and has no place for Tabrizian's ill-mannered and ignorant aggression which culminated in the act of book-burning.[39] For Ayatollah Arafi, scientific inquiry is essential to the pursuit of knowledge in Islamic traditions and is incompatible with an intellectual approach that refuses scholarly engagement from the beginning. The statement condemns the kind of Islamic tradition Tabrizian advocates. Similarly, Mostafa Rostami, President of the Association of the Leader's Office, voiced suspicions about Tabrizian's scholarly qualifications due to his poor scientific approach. He argues that one must be able to test one's own work from various angles and must not be too radical to claim the work to be scientific. Iran has succeeded in a variety of ways, precisely because, in his view, the country has safeguarded this (scientific) milieu to pursue knowledge. The foolish act of burning, he continues, is a big mistake and denigrates the fields of knowledge [science], intellect, and logic.[40] The reactions of these leaders against Tabrizian thus show that scientific inquiry is considered integral to their intellectual traditions and serves as a mainstream conceptual framework that is applied in various fields, including public health. Moreover, they criticized Tabrizian's act primarily because they regarded it to have failed to meet the scholarly standards of modern science. The reactions also reveal some distinct manners in which the conceptual framework of modern science is discussed, appraised, and verified by religious leaders. Overall, Tabrizian's controversy demonstrates that the status of modern science has risen among many religious leaders in Iran, but not without tensions,[41] given the popularity of Tabrizian in certain circles.

These tensions became more evident amid the outbreak. Tabrizian, despite the warning from the religious establishment in Iran, wrote a letter to the government, in which he presented a COVID-19 prescription based on Islamic medicine for the consideration of the Ministry of Health. The following prescription which appeared on his Telegram page has hardly, if any, resemblance to the one suggested by the Ministry of Health: (1) Do not leave foods and drinks without lids or plastic wrap; (2) Comb your

---

[39] https://etemadonline.com/content/379864/تعرض-اخیر-به-علم-پزشکی-جاهلانه-و-محکوم-است.

[40] https://etemadonline.com/content/379944/عباس-تبریزیان-کیست. See also Walbridge (2011) for fruitful discussions on Islamic logic and reasoning.

[41] See some similar cases in modern Iranian history explored in the works of Arjomand (1997), Mansouri (2013), Ringer (2001), and Schayegh (2009).

hair regularly; (3) Use brown sugar; (4) Eat onions a lot; (5) Eat apples a lot; (6) Take Imam Kazem medicine; (7) Sniff with medicines; (8) Dip a cotton ball in violet leaf oil and insert it in your anus; (9) Burn Peganum harmala; (10) Eat turnips a lot; (11) Give *ṣadaqe* (alms), especially breads; and (12) Buy Imam Kazem medicine from valid stores.[42] The number of his Telegram followers at that time was more than 128,000, and his Telegram messages can quickly spread and attract attention among a rather large audience. For example, one of his students showed up at local hospitals in different cities without protective gear and allegedly "treated" COVID-19 patients based on Islamic medicine. In the livestream he broadcasted, a student in clerical garb appeared to rub the patients' noses and mouths with Imam Kazem medicine.[43] Tabrizian's distrust of modern science has persisted throughout the outbreak, and he has continued disseminating messages that are at odds with the government's public health measures via social networking sites; for example, he expressed opposition to vaccination programs in the country, claiming on his Telegram account that the COVID-19 vaccines bring no cure to the disease but rather make those vaccinated homosexual.[44] Although his approaches and measures based on his reading of Islam are irrelevant and even laughable for many Iranians, they also disclose an uneasy strain embedded between modern science and Islam in Iran. This strain has the ability to impact on the effectiveness of public health measures, which are critical during a pandemic and rely on the commitment of the public.

Conclusion

This chapter looked at how the COVID-19 pandemic unfolded in Iran, a country in which state affairs operate under the checks of a religious establishment, and presented the kinds of activities, debates, and rationales that religious leaders engage in to confront the pandemic. From the early phase of the virus's upsurge, the Ministry of Health has been held accountable for handling public health measures, including disinfection, mask-wearing, and social distancing, and has been leading the efforts to curtail virus transmission at the national level. The Ministry of Health

[42] https://www.baharnews.ir/news/202389.

[43] http://www.ensafnews.com/223507/مدعی-طب-اسلامی-در-قرنطینه%E2%80%8Cی-بیمارستان/.

[44] https://www.hamshahrionline.ir/news/583545/ایجاد-گرایانه-همجنس-تمایلات-کرونا-واکسن-
ادعای-جدید-تبریزیان.

particularly draws upon modern science to understand the mechanism of virus transmission and to formulate public health guidelines therefrom. As a result, the field of public health is increasingly organized through a scientific paradigm, prompting religious leaders to become involved in conversations about the practical and theological implications of modern science.

Many religious leaders in Iran urgently call for the observance of the Ministry of Health's public health protocols during religious events that involve mass movement of participants, an indication that they find compelling the public health scheme laid out by modern science. Moreover, they attempt to adopt these schemes in ways that keep Islamic traditions meaningful and relevant for the faithful. Recent changes in some aspects of religious funerals during the pandemic are such an example. Under the pandemic, many more Iranians, both religious and non-religious, now turn to a virtual style of funeral while being attentive to both scientific health measures and Islamic teachings, an indication that science and Islam are interrelated and commensurable.

All religious leaders, however, do not agree with the ways in which scientific schemes are implemented in the fight against the virus. A self-proclaimed Ayatollah rejected scientific approaches in this fight and instead turned to Islamic medicine for curative guidance, characterizing modern science and Islam in antithetical terms. These emerging religious debates reveal some tensions in which Islamic traditions critically inform and are informed by the science-driven field of public health, the discussion of which is often, but cannot be, reduced to the terms of science only, especially in Iran. This chapter captures the shifting terrain of the relationship between modern science and Islam in Iran during the COVID-19 pandemic, this relationship being contingently conditioned by the discourses and practices surrounding the field of public health to which both modern science and Islam contribute in a distinctively historical manner.[45]

References

Abe, S. (2016). Management of the environment (mohit-e zist): An ethnography of Islam and environmental politics in Iran. *Japanese Review of Cultural Anthropology*, 17(1), 63–81.

---

[45] Elshakry (2013) examines the historically contingent ways in which modern science was uniquely introduced to Islamic contexts by tracing the debates about Darwin's *The Origin of Species* in the Arab world.

Abe, S. (2021). Pursuing moral dimensions of the environment: A study of Islamic tradition in contemporary Iran. *Journal for the Study of Religion, Nature and Culture*, 15(2), 151–176.

Arjomand, K. (1997). The emergence of scientific modernity in Iran: Controversies surrounding astrology and modern astronomy in the mid-nineteenth century. *Iranian Studies*, 30, 5–24.

Bayatrizi, Z., Ghorbani, H., and Tehrani, R.T. (2021). Risk, mourning, politics: Toward a transnational critical conception of grief for COVID-19 deaths in Iran. *Current Sociology*, 64(4), 512–528.

Behrouzan, O. (2016). *Prozak Diaries: Psychiatry and Generational Memory in Iran*, Stanford University Press.

Daston, L. (2000). (Ed.). *Biographies of Scientific Objects*, The University of Chicago Press.

Elshakry, M. (2013). *Reading Darwin in Arabic, 1860–1950*, The University of Chicago Press.

Esposito, J.L. (Ed.). (2004). *The Oxford Dictionary of Islam*, Oxford University Press.

Haeri, N. (2021). *Say What Your Longing Heart Desires: Women, Prayer & Poetry in Iran*, Stanford University Press.

Haider, N. (2014). *Shīʿī Islam: An Introduction*, Cambridge University Press.

Keddie, N. (2006). *Modern Iran: Roots and Results of Revolution*. New Haven, CT: Yale University Press.

Mansouri, R. (2013). The History of Science in Iran from a Physicist's Perspective. *Science and Innovations in Iran: Development, Progress, and Challenges*, ed. A. Soofi, Palgrave. pp. 15–38.

Mottahedeh, R. (1985). *The Mantle of the Prophet: Religion and Politics in Iran*, Oneworld Publications.

Najmabadi, A. (2014). *Professing Selves: Transsexuality and Same-Sex Desire in Contemporary Iran*, Duke University Press.

Pickering, A. (Ed.). (1992). *Science as Practice and Culture*, The University of Chicago Press.

Rahman, F. (1980). *Major Themes of the Qur'ān*, Bibliotheca Islamica.

Ringer, M. (2001). *Education, Religion, and the Discourses of Cultural Reform in Qajar Iran*, Mazda Publishers.

Schayegh, C. (2009). *Who is Knowledgeable is Strong: Science, Class, and the Formation of Iranian Society, 1900–1950*, University of California Press.

The Ministry of Health and Medical Education (2021). *Porotokol-e Behdāshtī Anvāʿ-ye Āzmūnhā* (Health Protocols for Exams).

Walbridge, J. (2011). *God and Logic in Islam: The Caliphate of Reason*, Cambridge University Press.

https://doi.org/10.1142/9789811253737_0008

Chapter 8

COVID-19 and Technology

Tai Wei Lim

Technology Comes to the Forefront

Prior to the outbreak of the COVID-19 pandemic, the world was engaged in intense Industry 4.0 and 5G technological competition with a determined US keen to maintain its technological lead in the world and China weaning off foreign imported technologies through the Made in China 2025 initiative. There was a lot of rhetoric and narratives from all tech powers about the future of technological development and the nature of technological competition.

However, when COVID-19 happened, the rhetoric and narratives soon became actual implementation and showcasing when the pandemic afforded all leading technological powers and their firms to put on display the most cutting-edge technologies in the world to fight the COVID-19 outbreak. Advanced robotics, telemedicine, tracking systems, and big data analytics were soon deployed to the frontlines of the battle against COVID-19. These sophisticated systems also became real-life displays of tech capabilities and strengths of each country and carry implications for the tech sector even after COVID-19 pandemic dies down eventually.

COVID-19 has revealed a number of vulnerabilities in humankind's defensive systems and the experience of the pandemic thus far has taught many the importance of technology in countering such disasters in the future. Smartphones and their killer apps have thus far provided real-time information and keep everyone in the know (although they are also responsible for spreading fake news, rumors, and panic as well).

Algorithms, Artificial Intelligence (AI), and data analytics have contributed to the capability of analyzing big data and creating predictive models to project the spread and proliferation of the virus. Start-up Yitu Technology, Huawei, and Alibaba are providing their AI-backed services to analyze computerized axial tomography (CAT) scans generated by hospitals to analyze COVID-19 suspect cases using the Tianhe-1 supercomputer to go through a few hundred CAT scan images and provide diagnosis (with claims of 80% accuracy) in approximately 10 seconds in the National Supercomputer Centre in Tianjin where the supercomputer is located.[1]

All these tools can make virus-coping mechanisms more effective and efficient. Online connectivity provide humankind with more effective means of understanding the proliferation, dangers, and properties of COVID-19 while proliferating safety messages, health slogans, and public campaigns. When the Spanish Flu hit the world in 1918, global communities did not have these sophisticated technologies to fight the humble virus.

Advanced Robotics and COVID-19

One category of advanced systems used to combat COVID-19 is the advanced robotics systems, and many tech powers rolled their latest hardware out for various functions in the global fight against the pandemic. Many robots work hand in hand with humans as human operators remotely maneuver them to clean up areas, move meals, beverages, and pharmaceuticals to people who need them, while others collect and supply data. There are also robots that contribute to psychological well-being by providing dancing companionship. But, perhaps, some of the most sophisticated robots are the autonomous systems that can disinfect areas without the need for human operators.

[1] Dai, Sarah (2020). "COVID-19: Chinese Government Launches New Tech Database to Help Communities Fight the Virus," *The Star*, accessed 17 March 2020, available at https://www.thestar.com.my/tech/tech-news/2020/03/17/covid-19-chinese-government-launches-new-tech-database-to-help-communities-fight-the-virus.

The mass media is filled with images of tech used for combating COVID-19 like Chinese police helmets infused with AI capabilities to identify individuals with fever at a distance of 16 feet away while, half a world away, another Los Angeles eatery monitors incoming customers' temperatures at the entrance with an infrared non-contact thermometer; and yet another accommodation facility near Houston's Texas Medical Center used robots to clean up and de-germ rooms and corridors.[2] China also deployed drones in the sky to monitor individuals who congregate outside to gossip or chat with each other and then use a loud hailer mounted on the drones to ask these perpetrators to go home, avoid congregation, and idle talk. The drones are also used to warn individuals to put on their masks through public identification (accompanied by a tinge of the element of public shame).

China was also busy deploying robotics system to combat the viral outbreak. In early March 2020, a field hospital known as the Smart Field Hospital manned by robots which can attend up to 20,000 patients was established in the Hongshan Sports Center in Wuhan China, the epicenter of the pandemic, by the Wuhan Wuchang Hospital, China Mobile and CloudMinds (a Sino-US cloud robotics systems manufacturer) to replace burnt-out medical workers.[3] The robots converted to manage COVID-19 outbreak include the humanoid Cloud Ginger (aka XR-1) and the Smart Transportation Robot which can move food and pharmaceutical supplies prescribed by physicians to those who need them as well as track the patient's critical readings, bypassing direct physical contact and Cloud Ginger can also provide individuals in confinement with news and entertainment contents.[4]

Aside from domestic deployment, the Americans are busy exporting their sophisticated robotics system overseas in the COVID-19 context. Texan Xenex Disinfection Services is accelerating production and

---

[2] Jolly, Jennifer (2020). "Coronavirus: The Role of Tech from Telemedicine to Star Trek-Like Devices," *USA TODAY*, accessed 18 March 2020, available at https://www.usatoday.com/story/tech/columnist/2020/03/18/coronavirus-tech-telemedicine-and-gadgets-war-against-covid-19/5058150002/.

[3] Hornyak, Tim (2020). "What America Can Learn from China's Use of Robots and Telemedicine to Combat the Coronavirus," *CNBC*, accessed 18 March 2020, available at https://www.cnbc.com/2020/03/18/how-china-is-using-robots-and-telemedicine-to-combat-the-coronavirus.html.

[4] *Ibid.*

despatching virus-killing robots to Singapore, Thailand, South Korea, Italy, and Houston, including the Xenex's LightStrike robots with germicidal UV light powered by concentrated pulsed xenon to disinfect dozens of rooms and common corridors daily by each robotic unit as well as emergency rooms, ambulances, and other areas with the presence of COVID-19 individuals.[5]

The Europeans are equally savvy with exporting their advanced robotics systems overseas. Odense Denmark-based UVD Robots dispatched hundreds of robots to the front-line workers in the battle against coronavirus. It has dispatched disinfection robots to Wuhan, Rome, and Veneto (Northern Italy) to shine a mounted all-round UV-C light ultraviolet light to decontaminate surfaces (about 9–10 rooms on the average, eliminating 99.9% bacteria and some viruses like MERS CoV and MHV-A59 in 10 minutes) and they are able to map out the physical surroundings in hospitals, operating autonomously with lidar navigation for approximately 2½ hours per charge.[6]

Besides terrestrially bound robots, flying drones are also utilized in the fight against COVID-19. China and Spain deployed drones to track individuals during city shutdowns, South Korea utilized robots to do deep disinfecting Daegu (an epicenter in South Korea) while Japanese drone manufacturer Antwork (a conglomerate of different companies) saw their Terra Drone flying and collecting medical samples and quarantine materials in Xinchang China in February 2020 at the peak of the viral outbreak.[7]

Social Distancing and Telemedicine Technology

The US has been using long-distance telemedicine technologies for years. Berkeley-based Eko built the FDA-approved digital stethoscope armed

---

[5] Jolly, Jennifer (2020). "Coronavirus: The Role of Tech from Telemedicine to Star Trek-Like Devices," *USA TODAY*, accessed 18 March 2020, available at https://www.usatoday.com/story/tech/columnist/2020/03/18/coronavirus-tech-telemedicine-and-gadgets-war-against-covid-19/5058150002/.

[6] *Ibid.*

[7] Hornyak, Tim (2020). "What America Can Learn from China's Use of Robots and Telemedicine to Combat the Coronavirus," *CNBC*, accessed 18 March 2020, available at https://www.cnbc.com/2020/03/18/how-china-is-using-robots-and-telemedicine-to-combat-the-coronavirus.html.

with an AI-powered cardiac screening platform for monitoring heartbeats and 40,000 have been sold from 2016 and implemented in 4,000 hospitals.[8] Besides measuring instruments, specialized video conferencing medical equipment have also been deployed for distant communications to prevent the spread of the COVID-19 disease. Nick Desai, CEO of Heal provides video calling devices combined with doctors' personal visits (deployable within a few hours from 8 in the morning till 8 in the evening) to their patients' accommodation, operating extensively in COVID-19-hit Silicon Valley in Northern California, New York City, and Seattle Washington.[9]

Heal can monitor respiration, heartbeat, pulse rate, and "live" vital signs readings that can act as a warning system for patients with tell-tale signs of health issues.[10] Minneapolis firm Zipnosis uses web-based questionnaires for patients to facilitate doctors' rapid differentiation of COVID-19 from other respiratory illnesses through asynchronous means with physicians reviewing the electronically submitted data using only an average of 1 minute 29 seconds to evaluate the patient and so only a few medical providers can manage over 400 visits per day.[11]

To prevent infected or potentially infected patients from turning up at clinics, community hospitals and polyclinics, doctors, health planners, and other stakeholders are trying to use technologies that can remotely connect these groups with doctors and medical practitioners so that they can treat the patients from afar. These can be derived from the existing telemedicine technologies. The US government is facilitating the use of these technologies by fast-tracking bureaucratic approval procedures. To facilitate the proliferation and implementation of tele-medicinal apps, the Trump administration modified federal rules to allow more physicians to treat their patients from a distance and encourage virtual consultations amidst the COVID-19 pandemic.[12]

---

[8] Jolly, Jennifer (2020). "Coronavirus: The Role of Tech from Telemedicine to Star Trek-Like Devices," *USA TODAY*, accessed 18 March 2020, available at https://www.usatoday.com/story/tech/columnist/2020/03/18/coronavirus-tech-telemedicine-and-gadgets-war-against-covid-19/5058150002/.

[9] *Ibid.*

[10] *Ibid.*

[11] *Ibid.*

[12] *Ibid.*

In Singapore, more than 500,000 users tap into the telehealth app MaNaDr established by general practitioner (GP) Dr. Siaw Tung Yeng with virtual patient consultation functions and now 20% of the Singaporean doctors dispense advisories through the app.[13] Some potential COVID-19 patients who were diagnosed this way are asked to home-quarantine if urgent medical attention is not required and they can also update their app doctors if they experience breathing difficulties, have sustained high fever, or generally deteriorate in health conditions and the physician can get an emergency vehicle to fetch them to a medical facility.[14]

Diagnosing patients online makes patients feel more at ease since they are within the comforts of their own homes and can prevent public medical facilities from being overwhelmed by patients, causing disruptions to the public healthcare system and infecting hospitals through a large concentration cluster of patients.[15] This is also in line with other anti-COVID-19 measures such as social distancing and stay-home calls to prevent more infections.

The Importance of Tracking Devices

Another category of devices used to combat, mitigate, and slow down virus spread are the medical tracking devices. Individuals going into the Smart Field Hospital in Hongshan Sports Center Wuhan China were monitored by 5G thermometers, which is an early warning system for patients with fever while patients/physicians/nurses wore smart bracelets and rings accessories connected to CloudMinds' AI platform so that crucial readings (like body temperature), heartbeat, and blood oxygen levels can be tracked at the initial stage of infection. Meanwhile, Chinese digital barcodes on smartphone apps can track and reveal the health status of individuals while older technologies like CCTV continue to monitor people leaving their apartments and Hong Kong residents compulsorily

---

[13] Park, Alice (2020). "The Tech That Could be Our Best Hope for Fighting COVID-19 and Future Outbreaks," *TIME*, accessed 19 March 2020, available at https://time.com/5805622/coronavirus-pandemic-technology/.

[14] *Ibid.*

[15] *Ibid.*

put on a wristband connected with a smartphone app to sound off authorities if an individual got out of her/his quarantine location.[16]

In India, another rising tech powerhouse and a large emerging economy like China, airplane and rail reservation information were tracked to prevent people from long-distance movement and, in Kerala (southern India), the state government utilized a combination of phone call logs, CCTV, and mobile app movement data to locate individuals who were proximate to COVID-19-stricken individuals.[17]

The large emerging economies and tech powers are not the only ones tapping into the rich treasure trove of data to fight the COVID-19 virus. The US Federal government is speaking to tech giants like Facebook (FB) and Google about the potential of tapping into their data to track the position and mobility data from the mobile phones of ordinary Americans for the purpose of dealing with COVID-19.[18] Meanwhile, medical practitioners in Israel utilize the 300 US dollars Tyto system to track individuals at a distance and Dr. Eyal Zimlichman (Chief Medical Officer and Chief Innovation Officer at Sheba Medical Center in Israel) and his teammates deployed the device to analyze almost a dozen people on the doomed COVID-19 infected British-registered Diamond Princess cruise ship that was docked in Yokohama Japan.[19]

Even smaller nation-states are tapping into these movement tracking technologies. The Singapore authorities, for example, uses the TraceTogether app based on Bluetooth communications between mobile phones to check if suspected COVID-19 vectors were proximate to other individuals while Republic of Korea (ROK) scans through credit card transactions, mobile movement data, CCTV and old-fashioned interviews to feed into a system where confirmed COVID-19 cases were constantly monitored and tracked, generating a map that reveal if certain individuals

---

[16] Kharpal, Arjun (2020). "Use of Surveillance to Fight Coronavirus Raises Concerns about Government Power after Pandemic Ends," CNBC.com, accessed 26 March 2020, available at https://www.cnbc.com/2020/03/27/coronavirus-surveillance-used-by-governments-to-fight-pandemic-privacy-concerns.html.

[17] *Ibid.*

[18] *Ibid.*

[19] Jolly, Jennifer (2020). "Coronavirus: The Role of Tech from Telemedicine to Star Trek-Like Devices," *USA TODAY*, accessed 18 March 2020, available at https://www.usatoday.com/story/tech/columnist/2020/03/18/coronavirus-tech-telemedicine-and-gadgets-war-against-covid-19/5058150002/.

had been near a COVID-19 vector.[20] To respect privacy, TraceTogether app does not take down position/location data or access the mobile owner's contact list while data logs are stored in encrypted format.[21]

All these technologies have proven to be extremely useful in combating the COVID-19 virus while tracing the infected victims. But there are also groups and individuals who are pushing back on such technological breakthroughs. For example, smartphones movement data have become a common tracking tool, leading to public backlash with some privacy advocates like non-profit organization (NPO) Electronic Frontier Foundation (EFF) arguing that state agencies should be prevented from sweeping rights to use such data unless they can demonstrate to the public that the methods help to combat COVID-19. This group opined that, while Global Positioning System (GPS)-based mobile systems are only readable up to a 16 feet radius (according to US government sources) but the Centers for Disease Control and Prevention (CDC) data indicated that COVID-19 can infect individuals in proximate contact within 6 feet, thus there are limitations and no guarantee that smartphone app-tracking technologies truly work.[22] The constant tensions between the tech advocates and the push-back resistance are likely to continue.

Unifying Applications

Meanwhile, states are not waiting for tech skeptics to voice their complete support as they forge ahead with plans to create consortiums and partnerships of multiple tech systems to have a consolidated tech approach in battling the COVID-19 disease. China is a good example of such consolidation of multiple systems. On 16 March 2020, the Ministry of Science and Technology announced that the Chinese bureaucracies have created a catalog of above 2,000 pioneering technologies (alongside their suppliers' names) ranging from auto temperature detection to diagnostics, affected communities, private-sector companies, foremost stakeholders in fighting

---

[20] Kharpal, Arjun (2020). "Use of Surveillance to Fight Coronavirus Raises Concerns about Government Power after Pandemic Ends," CNBC.com, accessed 26 March 2020, available at https://www.cnbc.com/2020/03/27/coronavirus-surveillance-used-by-governments-to-fight-pandemic-privacy-concerns.html.

[21] *Ibid.*

[22] *Ibid.*

the outbreak and hospital info systems, after its elite leaders emphasized the importance of a high-tech approach to tackling COVID-19.[23]

The first list of 283 technology products included systems for diagnosis and treatment of the virus, hospital information systems, logistical systems for ferrying crucial supplies and disinfection equipment and the objective of the list is to motivate more Chinese entities to take up and implement new tech systems in a prescribed and effective manner.[24] The eventual aim is to unify all the functions of different tech equipment and the acceleration of progress in research on life sciences/biotech/medical/healthcare machines in the same system, a process that is enhanced through Chinese President Xi's directive.[25]

Beijing is collectively managing 12 state departments to come up with treatment/cure, vaccines development, and the formulation of epidemiology and viral pathology models while President Xi met with the Politburo Standing Committee to announce the building of fresh infrastructures like the 5G networks and data centers in China recover faster from the pandemic.[26]

Collecting Big Data to Fight COVID-19

Long distance diagnosis is not new in even more advanced countries like the US which has already put in place machines that facilitates users to evaluate quantitatively indicators like temperature (especially rise in body temperatures within a certain area for cluster detection), blood pressure, and blood sugar levels throughout the day and the medical data is uploaded into cloud which can be drawn easily by physicians for medical evaluations.[27] When gathered in large quantities and protected appropriately by

---

[23] Dai, Sarah (2020). "COVID-19: Chinese Government Launches New Tech Database to Help Communities Fight the Virus," *The Star*, accessed 17 March 2020, available at https://www.thestar.com.my/tech/tech-news/2020/03/17/covid-19-chinese-government-launches-new-tech-database-to-help-communities-fight-the-virus.

[24] *Ibid.*

[25] *Ibid.*

[26] *Ibid.*

[27] Park, Alice (2020). "The Tech That Could be Our Best Hope for Fighting COVID-19 and Future Outbreaks," *TIME*, accessed 19 March 2020, available at https://time.com/5805622/coronavirus-pandemic-technology/.

confidentiality clauses, such data can become big data for predictive and macro diagnosis of entire groups or societies.

In the US, Kaiser Permanente tele-medicine call center's leader Dr. Stephen Parodi began tracking coronavirus-related phone calls from the 4.5-million-strong healthcare system in Northern California in February 2020 and his entries went from 200 to 3,500 phone calls daily about COVID-19, a tell-tale sign of community spread which was also indicative of an accelerated growth in the number of cases.[28] Based on the data collected, the hospitals are able to ascertain its suspension to make sure that the ventilators and other important COVID-19 treatment machines can be on standby for the projected large numbers of incoming severe COVID-19 patients and Kaiser's own medical practitioners can also turn away non-severe cases as well as routine check-ups (or make them virtual) in favor of serious COVID-19 cases.[29]

Jvion, a health analytics firm, utilizes AI to analyze 30 million patients in its database to highlight individuals and location most in danger of COVID-19 by using above 5,000 fields (such as medical track record, lifestyle choices, socioeconomic bases, housing issues, and transportation means) and then highlighting the individuals at risk based on the data collected so that they can be referred to healthcare providers.[30]

South Korea and Taiwan's successful use of technologies for identification, testing, and tracing are credited with quickly detecting isolated cases (Taiwan) and flattening out accelerated increases in infections (in the case of South Korea). Geo-tracking through phones and other devices helped South Korean trackers trace many individuals that the religious group Shinjicheon came into contact with. To respect the confidentiality and privacy that are vaunted in its liberal democratic system, the Republic of Korea (ROK) promises that the data collection efforts will terminate when the pandemic dies down and that all personal data collected will be erased.[31]

In Bangladesh, coding, computer programs, and algorithms originally created to track and monitor non-infectious illnesses such as hyper-

---

[28] *Ibid.*

[29] *Ibid.*

[30] *Ibid.*

[31] Kharpal, Arjun (2020). "Use of Surveillance to Fight Coronavirus Raises Concerns about Government Power after Pandemic Ends," CNBC.com, accessed 26 March 2020, available at https://www.cnbc.com/2020/03/27/coronavirus-surveillance-used-by-governments-to-fight-pandemic-privacy-concerns.html.

tension and diabetes are converted to include fields related to COVID-19 signs to accumulate big data about the proliferation of the virus and to allocate resources to fight it.[32] The strategic value of rapid detection is that one is able to delay or/and mitigate the pandemic peaking in order to prevent medical facilities from being overcrowded.

An important lesson to learn from this pandemic and is to further utilize technologies to their fullest potential. The pandemic may stimulate many in the medical establishment to change the way they practice medicine and reduce face-to-face consultations in the future, except for the most critical cases. The electronic inventory of pharmacies and sales of medicines like fever drugs may point to patterns and trends disease spread within the community.

Along with the use of these technologies to cope with viral outbreaks, other important issues like cybersecurity, confidentiality, and privacy are equally important. While these technologies help to facilitate convenience, speed, and efficiency for diagnosis, tracing, and treatment, the data accumulated from such procedures must be protected carefully. The more secure data management becomes, the more resources can be channeled easily to the right places with support from the people (social legitimacy for such measures).

Simple electronic measures can help to delay or replace radical measures such as quarantine or sealing off cities which can hurt the local communities' livelihoods and/or the national economy. Geotracking for example can give away location coordinates. It also provides hope for countries with less funding/finances and tracking infrastructures in the developing world to use smartphones for monitoring and accumulating data about epidemic clusters happening on the ground. In other words, the humble smartphones can be a source of affordable surveillance system to monitor the epidemic situation.

Lessons for the Future

Many are busy evaluating the current methods of handling COVID-19 with an eye on the future. COVID-19 may have just fast-tracked tech use to the forefront in the medical field. But at the same time, it has also been

[32] Park, Alice (2020). "The Tech That Could be Our Best Hope for Fighting COVID-19 and Future Outbreaks," *TIME*, accessed 19 March 2020, available at https://time.com/5805622/coronavirus-pandemic-technology/.

important to go through the proper procedures. One highly anticipated tech equipment currently undergoing approval by the US Food and Drug Administration (FDA) is the MedWan but the COVID-19 may just accelerate that process of approval.[33] Thus, legal and bureaucratic procedures may be short-circuited under the right emergency circumstances if certain safeguards are met, for example, the MedWan is armed with military-standard encryption to protect the data collected.[34]

With a machine the size of a small computer mouse, an inclusion of 10 medical diagnostic tools, and a hi-tech high-definition camera, the device MedWan facilitates the doctor's medical examination in an online platform by monitoring' one's heart and lungs, evaluating respiration/oxygen contents in blood, measuring body temperature, examining the skin, and looking into the tonsils with the data sent "live" to a protected video portal on the medical practitioner's computer.[35]

The trick for the successful implementation of all digital systems is to strike a balance between expediency in the use of data and protecting their privacy. Worries about privacy and confidentiality are real as some express anxieties over the prevalent use of such technologies to monitor the population even after COVID-19 is long gone, especially since some COVID-19-related collected data are also simultaneously fed into legal, judicial, and law enforcement systems. Israeli security firm Shin Bet is utilizing smartphone tracking data to recall where individuals have visited to implement quarantine measures and track the COVID-19 vectors, adding on to a non-disclosed backlog of data collected over the last few years for anti-terrorism objectives.[36] This has resulted in some public controversy in that country.

There are other examples of emerging technologies to cope with COVID-19 that respect privacy and confidentiality. The Massachusetts Institute of Technology (MIT) created the encrypted (off limits to unauthorized third parties) phone app "Private Kit: Safe Paths" to constantly

[33] Jolly, Jennifer (2020). "Coronavirus: The Role of Tech from Telemedicine to Star Trek-Like Devices," *USA TODAY*, accessed 18 March 2020, available at https://www.usatoday.com/story/tech/columnist/2020/03/18/coronavirus-tech-telemedicine-and-gadgets-war-against-covid-19/5058150002/.

[34] *Ibid.*

[35] *Ibid.*

[36] *Ibid.*

refresh personal data and indicate if they are stricken with COVID-19, along with locational data so that individuals can immediately receive signals when they are proximate to someone who has the virus while at the same time keeping the virus-hit individual's identity anonymous with privacy.[37]

[37] *Ibid.*

Part 4

COVID-19 and the Law

https://doi.org/10.1142/9789811253737_0009

Chapter 9

Legal Issues Pertaining to COVID-19 in Hong Kong

Samantha Ka Mei Ma

Introduction

It has been almost 2 years since the start of the COVID-19 pandemic. Hong Kong has done reasonably well in containing the spread of the pandemic in the city with the HKSAR government enacting regulations mandating the compulsory wearing of surgical masks, social distancing measures, quarantine, testing measures as well as the introduction of the voluntary vaccination program against COVID-19. The legal basis of these measures, which has been regularly under review, is mainly based on the Prevention and Control of Disease Ordinance (Cap 599) which balanced health concerns, economic impacts and social acceptance.

This chapter intends to cover a range of legal issues stemming from the COVID-19 pandemic in Hong Kong. There were voices of privacy concerns and discriminatory treatment of government healthcare measures. In the employment setting, the pandemic has brought severe financial hardships on businesses which in turn led to change in employment rights and conditions of employees. There have also been a number of cases in which Hong Kong courts were invited to examine issues of the constitutionality of wearing masks and the impact of COVID-19 on the duration of tenancy agreements.

Legal Issues Arising from the COVID-19 Pandemic in Hong Kong

Constitutionality of the regulation to mandate the wearing of surgical masks in specified public places

On 23 July 2020, the Chief Executive in Council under Section 8 of the Prevention and Control of Disease Ordinance (Cap 599) passed The Prevention and Control of Diseases (Wearing of Mask) Regulation (Cap 599I) which provided, *inter alia*, that "during a specified period, a person must wear a mask at all times when the person is entering or present in a specified public place." A fixed penalty of HK$5,000 was imposed on contravention of the offense.[1] This regulation has been a subject of judicial review in the Court of First Instance (CFI) of Hong Kong. In *Haider Ali v Social Welfare Department* [2020] HKFI 2611, the CFI found that the regulation was neither *ultra vires* nor unconditional by applying a four-step proportionality test, namely:

(1) The impugned measure pursues a legitimate aim, namely, the prevention or control of transmission of COVID-19.
(2) The impugned measure is rationally connected with the advancement of the legitimate aim.
(3) The impugned measure is not manifestly without reasonable foundation, and is no more than reasonably necessary for the purpose of advancing the legitimate aim.
(4) Having regard to the importance of the protection of public health, the impugned measure strikes a reasonable balance between (i) the societal benefits of the encroachment, and (ii) the restriction of the Applicant's liberty, i.e., the requirement to wear a mask in public places.[2]

---

[1] S6A of The Prevention and Control of Diseases (Wearing of Mask) Regulation (Cap 599I).

[2] *Haider Ali v Social Welfare Department* [2020] HKFI 2611, para 9.

With the constitutionality of wearing surgical masks confirmed in Hong Kong court, and the general consensus and understanding of Hong Kong people on wearing surgical masks to curb the spread of COVID-19, wearing surgical masks has been a part of life of all Hong Kong people during the pandemic, and may be beyond.

Discrimination and COVID-19

The Equal Opportunities Commission (EOC) of Hong Kong is responsible for implementing the four anti-discrimination ordinances in Hong Kong, namely the Sex Discrimination Ordinance (SDO), the Disability Discrimination Ordinance (DDO), the Family Status Discrimination Ordinance (FSDO), and the Race Discrimination Ordinance (RDO). It has addressed issues of concern of the public on potential cases of discrimination relating to COVID-19.[3]

During the early phase of the COVID-19 pandemic, there were cases of potential discriminatory practices reported to the EOC. The EOC has urged the Hong Kong public to approach the matter with "reason and empathy."[4] One of which was that a restaurant posted a notice that it refused to serve customers who are the participants of Universal Community Testing Programme (UCTP). The management of the restaurant may be under an assumption that these customers are likely to have been infected with COVID-19. The EOC found the practice of the restaurant not to be on reasonable grounds and was not "reasonably necessary" for the purpose of public health and is likely to be unlawful under DDO, with the restaurant viewing infection with COVID-19 as a "disability" under DDO. The EOC strongly condemned the practice of the restaurant as discriminatory.[5] However, with the growing awareness and knowledge of Hong Kong people of the COVID-19 and the means of prevention of

---

[3] Press Release of Equal Opportunities Commission of Hong Kong (2021). "EOC Responds to Media Enquiries," 14 April, available at https://www.eoc.org.hk/en/PressRelease/Detail/17238.

[4] Press Release of Equal Opportunities Commission of Hong Kong (2020). "EOC Urges Reason and Empathy in Dealing with People and Facilities Related to the Novel Coronavirus," 11 February, available at https://www.eoc.org.hk/en/PressRelease/Detail/16520.

[5] Press Release of Equal Opportunities Commission (2020). "EOC Responds to Media Enquiries," 31 August, available at https://www.eoc.org.hk/en/PressRelease/Detail/16861.

the spread thereof, such discriminatory practice which only appeared in very rare cases and in the early phase of the COVID-19 pandemic has disappeared.

There is another potential discriminatory practice related to the COVID-19 vaccination program. On the potential discriminatory impact of requiring employees to be vaccinated against COVID-19 or they may be dismissed, EOC commented that "this requirement may have a greater adverse impact on those people who are not suitable for vaccination, such as people with serious illnesses or pregnant women. Unless the employer has reasonable grounds to support the requirement, it may constitute indirect discrimination on the grounds of disability or pregnancy." COVID-19 vaccination remains a voluntary decision though the Hong Kong government and local businesses have created various incentives to encourage people to get vaccinated.[6]

A further potential discriminatory measure by the Hong Kong Government is the mandatory scanning of QR code with the "LeaveHomeSafe" app from 1 November 2021 on entering government premises as there are socially disadvantaged who may not be able to afford a mobile phone. The elderly may also not be able to use a mobile phone to scan the QR code. Such measures discouraged them from entering government premises such as public libraries and public sports centers or even the government-managed wet markets. In response to the potential "digital discrimination," Ricky Chu, Chairman of Equal Opportunities Commission, said the new rule does not breach any anti-discrimination laws as it concerns electronic devices but advised that the law enforcement agencies should use "common sense" in its enforcement of the new rule.[7]

While we treasure a community that caters for equal treatment for all and we oppose discriminatory treatment, the COVID-19 pandemic is novel and unprecedented so it is understandable that people has guarded against people being potentially infected with COVID-19 at the early phase of the pandemic. With the passage of time when Hong Kong people

[6] HKSAR Press Release, "Early Vaccination for All," available at https://www.covidvaccine.gov.hk/en/programme.

[7] *South China Morning Post* (2021). "Hong Kong's 'Leave Home Safe' Mandate Amounts to Differential Treatment, Equality Watchdog Chief Warns," 23 October, available at https://www.scmp.com/news/hong-kong/politics/article/3153460/hong-kongs-leave-home-safe-mandate-amounts-differential.

has come to live with COVID-19 as the "new normal," discriminatory practice is fading.

Employment Law and COVID-19

During the early phase of the pandemic in Hong Kong, many employees were asked to work from home or to take no-pay leave. There were a host of employment issues relating to the COVID-19 pandemic. Hence, the Labour Department of Hong Kong has published a pamphlet titled "Obligations and rights of employers and employees under the Employment Ordinance relating to the Coronavirus Disease 2019" which detailed the rights and obligations of employers and employees in relation to employees contracting COVID-19, employees subjecting to quarantine, employee receiving vaccination, and undergoing COVID-19 testing.[8]

In cases where an employee contracted COVID-19 unrelated to employment, he shall be granted sick-leave in accordance with the Employment Ordinance (EO) and his employment contract. If an employee is required to undergo quarantine, he shall be entitled to sick leave certificates, and sick leave allowance (if appropriate) upon submission of proof of their stay at the quarantine center issued by the Department of Health.

In the heat of the COVID-19 pandemic in 2020, some employees were requested to take no-pay leave. The Labour Department clarified that there is no statutory regulation on no-pay leave. In cases where the business suffers difficulties in operation because of the pandemic, it urged the employers and employees to discuss the mutually agreed arrangement taking into account the needs of individual employees.[9]

A related employment issue is the requirement for COVID-19 vaccination program as an employee, while vaccination remains a voluntary decision in Hong Kong. On 1 September 2021, Cathay Pacific Airlines, the largest Airline in Hong Kong, implemented a fully vaccinated crew. It thus sacked a few employees because they failed to take the

---

[8] Labour Department (2021). "Obligations and Rights of Employers and Employees under the Employment Ordinance Relating to the Coronavirus Disease 2019," July, available at https://www.labour.gov.hk/eng/news/pdf/EO_related_QAs_on_COVID-19_eng.pdf.
[9] *Ibid.*

COVID-19 vaccine by the deadline set by the company and failed to provide medical proof of their unsuitability of taking the vaccine.[10] It is a sensible management decision of such a big Airline which needs to serve the Hong Kong and international travelers while posing limited adverse effect on the employees.

In 2020, Hong Kong has 373,884 Foreign Domestic Helpers (FDH), so the issue of their rights and obligations of their employers is an important concern.[11] On 23 March 2020, the Hong Kong government denied entry to Hong Kong for all non-Hong Kong residents coming from overseas countries and regions by plane with effect from 25 March 2020. However, an exemption has been granted to the FDH who plan to come to Hong Kong to commence a new contract or continue the current contract after vacation leave in his/her place of origin, though they are still subject to quarantine arrangements as other Hong Kong residents returnees.[12]

To address the potential employment issue of FDH, in December 2020, the Labour Department published the pamphlet "Obligations and Rights of Employers and Foreign Domestic Helpers under the Employment Ordinance and Standard Employment Contract and Other Information relating to Coronavirus Disease (COVID-19)."[13] It clarified that the employers have to bear the accommodation expenses incurred by the FDH and the provision of food allowance in undergoing compulsory quarantine upon entry in Hong Kong. On the wages of FDH under compulsory quarantine, the Labour Department clarified that there is no provision in the Employment Ordinance but it encouraged

---

[10] *The Standard* (2021). "Hammer Falls on Cathay Pacific No-Jab, No-Excuse Cabin Crew," 9 September, available at https://www.thestandard.com.hk/section-news/section/11/234045/Hammer-falls-on-Cathay-Pacific-no-jab,-no-excuse-cabin-crew.

[11] Immigration Department of Hong Kong (2021). "Statistics on the Number of Foreign Domestic Helpers in Hong Kong (English)," 25 February, available at https://data.gov.hk/en-data/dataset/hk-immd-set4-statistics-fdh/resource/063e1929-107b-47ae-a6ac-b4b1ed460ac3.

[12] HKSAR Press Release (2020). "Government Announces Enhancements to Anti-Epidemic Measures in Four Aspects," 24 March, available at https://www.info.gov.hk/gia/general/202003/24/P2020032400050.htm.

[13] Labour Department of Hong Kong (2020). "Obligations and Rights of Employers and Foreign Domestic Helpers under the Employment Ordinance and Standard Employment Contract and Other Information relating to Coronavirus Disease (COVID-19)" December 2020, available at https://www.fdh.labour.gov.hk/res/pdf/obligations_and_rights_of_employers_and_fdhs_en.pdf.

employers "to be considerate and show understanding to such employees' situation and make flexible arrangements."[14] In case an FDH contracted COVID-19, he/she shall be entitled to sick leave and sick allowance as any other sickness, as stipulated for in the EO. The Labour Department cautioned employers not to dismiss the FDH because he/she contracted COVID-19 as it may constitute unfair dismissal.

One particular concern in relation to FDH is that it is a normal practice among FDH to have group gatherings, food sharing, and other social activities on their rest days, normally Sundays, in various parks in Hong Kong. Noting the inherent risks of spread of COVID-19 in these activities, the Labour Department has repeatedly issued press releases to advise FDH to wear surgical masks and to refrain from gathering in public places and staying in crowded places on rest days.[15] Nevertheless, the Labour Department also reminded the employers that it will contravene the Employment Ordinance if the FDH is deprived of his/her rest days. Thanks to the efforts of Hong Kong community and the FDH in Hong Kong, there has never been a widespread outbreak of COVID-19 among FDH group gatherings.[16]

In February 2022, the HKSAR government introduced the Employment (Amendment) Bill 2022 to provide a legal response to employment issues arising from COVID-19.[17]

It stipulates for, *inter alia*, two new provisions. Section 32KA provides that an employee who is absent from work due to compliance with a requirement with restriction on movement imposed under the Prevention and Control of Disease Ordinance (Cap 599) will be deemed as sickness days under the EO. It is not a valid reason to dismiss an employee or vary the terms of an employee's employment contract on the ground of the employee being an affected employee. Section 32KB of the Bill further provides that dismissal of employee's non-compliance of

---

[14] *Ibid.*, p. 7.

[15] HKSAR Press Release (2020). "Government Appeals to Foreign Domestic Helpers and Members of the Public to Comply with Anti-Epidemic Regulations and Measures on Prohibition of Group Gatherings of More Than Two Persons and Mask-Wearing in Public Places (with Photos)," 27 December, available at https://www.info.gov.hk/gia/general/202012/27/P2020122700738.htm.

[16] Infra note 14, p. 10.

[17] Employment (Amendment) Bill 2022 was gazette on 25 February 2022, available at https://www.gld.gov.hk/egazette/pdf/20222673e/es3202226734.pdf.

the vaccination requirement of the "vaccine pass" scheme under the law (Cap 599L) or failure to produce proof of having vaccinated of any COVID-19 vaccine recognized by the HKSAR government after request being made by the employer by the expiry of a specified period constitutes a valid reason for dismissal under the EO, except that the employee can provide medical reason for exemptions of vaccinations. This government said the Bill will have a sunset clause which will be repealed when the COVID-19 pandemic is under control and vaccination is no longer a matter of public health concern.[18]

In the employment setting, while it is understandable that the employers who are business owners have been under severe financial assault in the COVID-19 pandemic, the employees' livelihood and income have also been severely affected. While the existing employment ordinance has been developed over the years to cater to the respect of rights and obligations of the employers and employees, the COVID-19 pandemic has presented new legal challenges to the relationship which needs flexibility and understanding of both parties to reshape the mutual rights and obligations in the midst of the pandemic.

Tenancy dispute and COVID-19

Many businesses suffered severely as a result of the onset of the COVID-19 with many government healthcare measures to stem the spread of COVID-19. There were several Hong Kong court cases in which the tenants argued that COVID-19 is a "frustrating event," a principle of contract law which entitled the contractual party to seek early termination of the tenancy agreement. A tenant has also invited the Court to consider whether it has power to reduce the rent of the tenancy.

In *Holdwin Ltd v Prince Jewellery and Watch Co Ltd* (HCA 718/2020, 414/2021), the tenancy defaulted in payments of rent so the landlord sought for a summary judgment on the arrears of rent. The tenant argued that COVID-19 pandemic was a frustrating event as its businesses suffered financially with the drop of tourists and overseas visitors, so it

[18] HKSAR Press Release (2022). "Employment (Amendment) Bill 2022 Gazetted Today," 25 February, available at https://www.info.gov.hk/gia/general/202202/25/P2022022500732.htm.

entitled the tenant to terminate the tenancy. The CFI, first referred to the general principle of frustration in Chitty on Contracts:

> As a general rule, a contract may be discharged on the ground of frustration when something occurs after the formation of the contract which (1) renders it physically or commercially impossible to fulfil the contract or (2) transforms the obligation to perform into a radically different obligation from that undertaken at the moment of entry into the contract.[19]

The Court then referred to two previous Hong Kong cases, *The Centre Ltd v Victory Serviced Office (HK) Ltd* [2020] HKCFI 2991 and *Sunbroad Holdings Ltd v A Paris HK Ltd* [2021] HKCFI 1422 in which both Courts held that the COVID-19 pandemic and the social disruption in 2019 in Hong Kong did not "fundamentally change the nature of the outstanding contractual rights and/or obligations from what the parties reasonably contemplated at the time of the execution of the tenancy agreement."[20] The CFI found that it is "extremely rare" that the doctrine of frustration would apply to leases.[21] The CFI, concurring the decision of the two other cases, held that COVID-19 pandemic is not a frustrating event which entitled the tenant to terminate the tenancy agreement prematurely. The decision of the CFI of Hong Kong in *Holdwin Ltd v Prince Jewellery and Watch Co Ltd* is a welcomed decision which affirmed that COVID-19, though unprecedented, is a fact of commercial world. "The vicissitudes of economic fortune must have been an event that the Defendant, as a commercial entity, has to face," the Court said.[22]

Failing to terminate the contract because of frustration, the tenant may like to negotiate the reduction of rent in the midst of the COVID-19 pandemic. In *何漢超 v Chong Chi Ki Pierre* [2021] HKCA 1652, the tenant argued on appeal, *inter alia*, that

> The courts are empowered by law to make rental adjustments during the COVID-19 pandemic. The Judge should have considered the actual situation in Hong Kong including the impact of the pandemic, and adjusted

[19] *Holdwin Ltd v Prince Jewellery and Watch Co Ltd* (HCA 718/2020, 414/2021), para 23.
[20] *Ibid.*, para 28.
[21] *Ibid.*, para 32.
[22] *Ibid.*, para 43.

the rent according to the latest rateable valuation of the premise, and gave relief against forfeiture under section 21F of the High Court Ordinance, Cap. 4.[23]

The tenant relied on a document on rent concession of Hong Kong Housing Authority on non-domestic tenancies but the Court found that it is irrelevant as the tenancy in question is a domestic tenancy. The tenant further relied on an Australian case of *Sneakerboy*[24] which concerns relief against to a tenant following the termination of a retail lease during the COVID-19 pandemic, in which the Australian regime was said to have imposed "a set of good faith leasing principles for between landlords and commercial tenants."[25] The Court rejected this argument as it said that Hong Kong does not have an equivalent of the Australian COVID-regime or regulation. The Court found that it has no power to order rent reduction or rent waivers as it is up to the landlord and tenant to agree among themselves. The Court has no power to intervene in the contract between the landlord and tenant, whether for domestic or commercial tenancies.[26] A tenancy is a freely negotiated contract between two parties on equal footing. The terms of the tenancy, including the rent or reduction thereof, should ultimately be left to be agreed between the parties. In fact, there have been many cases where the landlord has agreed to rent reduction to tenants so that the tenant can survive the difficult economic downturn.

The COVID-19 pandemic has also led to the termination of a tenancy by a landlord. In March 2020, a Chinese restaurant in Hong Kong had a COVID-19 cluster outbreak, which was believed to be a short-distance airborne transmission. Experts found that the fresh air transmission was only one-third of the normal standard and the ventilation of the restaurant was very poor which resulted in cross-infection at different tables.[27] While the terms of the tenancy and the grounds for the termination of tenancy

---

[23] *何漢超 v Chong Chi Ki Pierre* [2021] HKCA 1652, at para 14.

[24] *Sneakerboy Retail Pty Ltd (t/as Sneakerboy) v Georges Properties Pty Ltd* [2020] NSWSC 996.

[25] Infra note 20, para 22.

[26] *Ibid.* para 18, 23.

[27] Hong Kong Standard (2021). "K11 Musea to Terminate Contract of COVID-Hit Restaurant after it Failed to Meet Hygiene Standards," 2 March, available at https://www.thestandard.com.hk/breaking-news/section/4/166525/K11-Musea-to-terminate-contract-of-Covid-hit-restaurant-after-it-failed-to-meet-hygiene-standards.

was not disclosed publicly in the media, it remains a sensible decision on the part of both parties to terminate the tenancy on the basis of public health concern and commercial reality.

As an effort to give short term rent relief to tenants, the Financial Secretary proposed in his annual budget speech in February 2022–2023 a "rent enforcement moratorium' which deters the landlords from termination of tenancies or other legal enforcement of non-payment of rent of the tenants for 3 months period subject to extension but the legislation will be lapsed after 6 months.[28] Such initiative has been met by mixed response from the business community. Hong Kong Retail Management Association and Hong Kong Federation of Restaurants and Related Trades welcomed such proposal as it can help businesses deeply hurt by COVID-19. However, Legislator Louis Loong Hon-biu who represents the real estate and construction sector, said that the proposal was based on the misconception that landlords are always better off than the tenants. Instead, he said some landlords may face cashflow problems in paying mortgage if they fail to collect rent.[29] Having listened to the voices of the business community, the Financial Secretary conceded that the rent enforcement moratorium will only be valid for 3 months, saying that it hopes landlord and tenants can renegotiate their rental arrangements in these difficult times. He also suggested lending a maximum sum of HK$100,000 as a 3-month rent for the elderly landlord who relied on rental income for a living.[30] Such initiative has yet to be debated in the legislative council. It remains a difficult decision for the government to strike a balance between protecting the interests of the landlords and tenants.

Personal data privacy concern

Personal data privacy is not an absolute right. It may be subjected to other competing interests and rights. One prominent issue in the COVID-19 pandemic is the need to balance the public interests of health and safety of the community, and the use of personal data of citizens. Article 59 of the Personal Data (Privacy) Ordinance (Cap 486) stipulates an exemption

---

[28] "2022–2023 Budget of HKSAR Government," paragraph 171, 23 February 2022, available at https://www.budget.gov.hk/2022/eng/budget48.html.

[29] *South China Morning Post* (2022). "Protection Period' for Rental Waiver Scheme Now Halved," 8 March.

[30] *Ibid.*

from a data protection principle of obtaining prescribed consent of data subject of personal data if it relates to the physical or mental health of the data subject. Section 60B of the Ordinance further provides for an exemption if the data are required by law. The principal regulation in the COVID-19 setting is The Prevention and Control of Disease (Disclosure of Information) Regulation (Cap 599D). Notwithstanding these regulations in place, the applicability of data protection principle in the COVID-19 setting remains a delicate exercise.

From mid-March 2020 onward, inbound travelers to Hong Kong who have to undergo compulsory quarantine have to wear wristbands and download a mobile app "StayHomeSafe" to verify that they are staying in their dwelling places for compulsory quarantine. The Government Chief Information Officer has dispelled the privacy concern of the tracking device.[31] The wristbands do not contain GPS device while the mobile app does not collect geo-location data. They only aim is to confirm that a person is staying at home by analyzing environmental communication signals such as Bluetooth, Wi-Fi, and geospatial signals.

The HKSAR government also introduced the online dashboard to list the buildings in which the confirmed or probable infection cases have been found.[32] It balances privacy concern and information transparency by only disclosing the gender and age of the patients but does not contain data that are precise enough to identify the infected person.

In November 2020, HKSAR government launched the Launch of "LeaveHomeSafe" COVID-19 exposure notification mobile app. It records the time for the checking in and leaving specific premises by scanning the venue QR code such that, if a COVID-19 case is discovered in the premises, the app user can be alerted.[33] From March 2021, the HKSAR government gradually required the scanning of the QR code with the app upon entry into the government premises and restaurants, leaving the option for people to fill in a paper record of their date and time of visit of the said premises. However, from 1 November 2021, all government

---

[31] "Wristbands Pose no Privacy Issue," 18 March 2020, available at https://www.news.gov.hk/eng/2020/03/20200318/20200318_232832_530.html.

[32] Online Dashboard of the Latest Situation of Novel Coronovirus Infection in Hong Kong, available at https://chp-dashboard.geodata.gov.hk/covid-19/en.html.

[33] "Launch of 'LeaveHomeSafe' COVID-19 Exposure Notification Mobile App (with Photos)," Press Release of HKSAR, 11 November 2020, available at https://www.info.gov.hk/gia/general/202011/11/P2020111100367.htm.

employees and members of the public will be required to use the app to scan the venue QR code before they are allowed to enter government buildings or offices, subject to limited exemptions.[34]

On the introduction of the "LeaveHomeSafe" app by the HKSAR government, there were voices of privacy concern in the general public.[35] According to the privacy policy of the app, it only collects personal data with the user's consent and this data may include name, telephone number, e-mail address, visit records, identity document number, COVID-19 vaccination records, and testing results. The authorities indicated that the data are only used for exposure notifications to app users and help facilitating the work of the HKSAR Government in controlling the spread of COVID-19. Personal data will not be kept longer than is reasonably necessary for the purpose for which it is collected.[36]

To dispel the privacy concern, the HKSAR government clarified that:

> (It) upholds the principle of protecting personal data privacy, and user registration is not required. The app will not use positioning services or any other data of the users' mobile phones. Venue check-in data will be encrypted and saved on users' devices only. Such data will not be uploaded to the Government or any other systems. Check-in data will be kept in users' mobile phones for 31 days and will then be erased automatically.[37]

Perhaps because of the privacy concern, some people risk downloading a counterfeit version of "LeaveHomeSafe" app. On the first day of the strict enforcement of scanning of QR code with "LeaveHomeSafe" app upon entry of government buildings in November 2021, five persons were arrested for scanning the QR code with a counterfeit version of "LeaveHomeSafe" app and were charged with the offense of using false

---

[34] "Strict Enforcement of Requirement of Using 'LeaveHomeSafe' Mobile Application when Entering Government Buildings or Offices," available at https://www.info.gov.hk/gia/general/202110/21/P2021102100647.htm, 21 October 2021.

[35] RTHK (2021). "Hospital Union 'Spreading Unfounded Info about App,'" 19 February, available at https://news.rthk.hk/rthk/en/component/k2/1576429-20210219.htm?spTabChangeable=0.

[36] Privacy Policy of "Leave Home Safe" app, available at https://www.leavehomesafe.gov.hk/en/privacy/.

[37] Infra note 33.

documents, an offense that carries a maximum sentence of 14 years' jail on conviction.[38]

On the data privacy concern in the employment setting, the Office of the Privacy Commissioner for Personal Data, Hong Kong, recommended that the employers may, on the principle that it is "necessary, appropriate and proportionate," collect personal data of the employees such as health data and travel history to help contain the spread of the virus.[39]

The Office of the Privacy Commissioner for Personal Data has reiterated time and again that the right to privacy is not an absolute right. The COVID-19 pandemic has shown that many privacy rights of Hong Kongers have been hindered in favor of the overwhelming concern for public health. But, as the COVID-19 pandemic is a global health issue, the encroachment of privacy right of citizens in the name of the public health reason has received general support of Hong Kong citizens.

Indemnity fund for adverse events following immunization with Coronavirus Disease-2019 vaccines

In order to protect individuals from contacting COVID-19 and to reduce the seriousness of its symptoms after catching it, the HKSAR government introduced two vaccines for the public: CoronaVac COVID-19 Vaccine and Comirnaty COVID-19 mRNA Vaccine. By 31 August 2021, there were about 7,588,200 doses of COVID-19 vaccines administered with a reporting rate of 0.07% of Adverse Events Following Immunization ("AEFIs").[40] The HKSAR government also launched the Indemnity Fund for Adverse Events Following Immunization with Coronavirus Disease-2019 Vaccines to provide financial support to those suffering

---

[38] *South China Morning Post* (2021). "Coronavirus Hong Kong: 5 Arrested for Using Fake Version of 'Leave Home Safe' App as Mandatory Rules Kick in: Government Staff among those Held," 1 November, available at https://www.scmp.com/news/hong-kong/health-environment/article/3154417/coronavirus-hong-kong-5-arrested-using-fake.

[39] Office of the Privacy Commissioner for Personal Data (2020). "Fight COVID-19 Pandemic Guidelines for Employers and Employees," 30 March, available at https://www.pcpd.org.hk/english/news_events/media_statements/press_20200330.html.

[40] Drug Office, Department of Health of HKSAR Government (2021). "Safety Monitoring of COVID-19 Vaccines in Hong Kong" 3 September, available at https://www.drugoffice.gov.hk/eps/do/en/doc/Safety_Monitoring_of_COVID-19_Vaccines_in_Hong_Kong.pdf, p. 5.

from AEFIs.[41] The maximum payout for deaths associated with serious adverse effects of vaccines is HKD2,500,000 while those for injuries is HKD3,000,000.[42]

At the point of writing this chapter, the Indemnity Fund has not found any deaths associated with serious adverse effects of vaccines. In November 2021, the Coroner's Court heard the first case of death of a man who died two days after taking CoronaVac COVID-19 Vaccine. He has pre-existing medical conditions including hypertension, high cholesterol, and high blood sugar, as well as diabetes and problems with heart arteries. The autopsy report found that the man died of a lung condition triggered by a heart condition. The Jury ruled that his death was an open verdict as they believed that there were other factors other than heart condition which triggered the lung condition.[43] Notwithstanding the Coroner's court decision, the arbiter of the release of Indemnity Fund was in the hands of the Expert Committee which has ruled that the death of the 63-year old man was not associated with serious adverse effects of vaccines.

An issue relating to the vaccination is the vaccine pass introduced by HKSAR government on 24 February 2022. The Secretary for Food and Health (SFH) issued "Vaccine Pass direction" (the Direction) in accordance with the Prevention and Control of Disease (Vaccine Pass) Regulation (Cap 599L) which provides that the Vaccine Pass will be applicable to all catering business premises and scheduled premises specified in the Direction under the Prevention and Control of Disease (Requirements and Directions) (Business and Premises) Regulation (Cap 599F). Under the Vaccine Pass arrangement, all persons entering or remaining on any catering business premises or specified premises are required to carry an electronic or a paper copy of their COVID-19 vaccination record or Exemption Certificate and made them available for inspection.[44]

---

[41] Indemnity Fund for Adverse Events Following Immunization with Coronavirus Disease-2019 Vaccines, available at https://www.axa.com.hk/en/aefi-fund.

[42] *Ibid.*

[43] *The Standard* (2021). "Death of 63-Year-Old Man who Died Two Days after Getting Sinovac Ruled as Open Verdict," 12 November.

[44] HKSAR Press Release (2021). "Government Announces Implementation Arrangements for Vaccine Pass," 21 February, available at https://www.info.gov.hk/gia/general/202202/21/P2022022100781.htm.

While the HKSAR government introduced the vaccine pass arrangement as a matter of public health concern, there are people who refuse to get vaccinated. There are a few court cases in which people initiated judicial review against the government's decision to introduce the vaccine pass arrangement.[45] In one case, the claimant Ms. Law stated in the writ that the vaccine pass arrangement prevented her from applying for the property agent license exams and hence lost her job opportunities. It also deterred her from entering wet markets and supermarkets to buy daily necessities. She was also forced to buy takeaway and was being denied access to all public facilities.[46] The High Court of Hong Kong ruled against the claimant, holding that the vaccine pass arrangement has already bore a reasonable balance between protection of public health and the individual right of citizens of access to public facilities and daily needs. The court noted in particular the fact that Hong Kong is a "geographically small, densely populated, and highly urbanized area with a high level of mobility." So, the measure aims at encouraging unvaccinated people to get vaccinated and to reduce the presence of unvaccinated people in locations where COVID-19 is likely to be transmitted.[47]

As World Health Organization stated that "effective vaccines is critical to ending the COVID-19 pandemic,"[48] it is encouraging that with HKSAR government policies and businesses incentives, the vaccination rate of the first dose of vaccine has reached 92.3% of the population as of 6 April 2022.[49]

Concluding Remarks

The COVID-19 pandemic has brought about novel legal issues, with public health concerns at the core of such issues, including the possibility of

[45] *The Standard* (2022). "Second Citizen Files Judicial Review against Vaccine Pass," 21 February, available at https://www.thestandard.com.hk/breaking-news/section/4/187380/Second-citizen-files-judicial-review-against-vaccine-pass.

[46] *The Standard* (2022). "Judicial Review against Vaccination Pass Thrown out by High Court," 30 March, available at https://www.thestandard.com.hk/breaking-news/section/4/188689/Judicial-review-against-vaccination-pass-thrown-out-by-High-Court.

[47] *Ibid.*

[48] World Health Organization, "COVID-19 Vaccines," available at https://www.who.int/emergencies/diseases/novel-coronavirus-2019/covid-19-vaccines.

[49] Infra note 33.

infringing or limiting the rights of citizens. The HKSAR government has striven to balance the needs of healthcare concern with the voices from the public on the infringement of citizens' rights. Private citizens also were required to reexamine and renegotiate their rights and obligations in the business and employment setting in light of the pandemic. The Hong Kong courts have ruled on various disputes between litigants on the change in legal relations because of the onset of COVID-19 pandemic.

It has been more than 2 years since the start of the COVID-19 pandemic and the world is still struggling with it. Thanks to the release of various COVID-19 vaccines and the recent news of Pfizer's antiviral treatment, "PAXLOVID" which claimed to have reduced the death rate and hospitalization rate by 89%.[50] It is hoped that the COVID-19 pandemic is on the road to be under control.

[50] Pfizer, "Pfizer's Novel COVID-19 Oral Antiviral Treatment Candidate Reduced Risk of Hospitalization or Death By 89% in Interim Analysis of Phase 2/3 Epic-HR Study," available at https://www.pfizer.com/news/press-release/press-release-detail/pfizers-novel-covid-19-oral-antiviral-treatment-candidate.

Part 5

COVID-19 and Global Trade

https://doi.org/10.1142/9789811253737_0010

Chapter 10

The Maritime Silk Road (MSR) in the Era of COVID-19 Coronavirus Pandemic*

Tai Wei Lim

Introduction

Started in 2013 by the Xi administration, China has sunk more than 450 billion US dollars in Belt and Road Initiative (BRI) connectivity infrastructure projects in almost 140 countries in the Asian, European, South American, and African continents to open up new markets.[1] The Maritime Silk Road (MSR) makes up 50% of international trade between China/East Asia and Europe facilitated by the globe's biggest container ports in Shanghai, Singapore, Shenzhen, Ningbo-Zhoushan, Busan, and Hong Kong.[2] In the MSR, Chinese companies like COSCO and China Merchants Group operate port terminals in the globe's five most notable

---

* This chapter is drawn from a small section of the author's manuscript on the Maritime Silk Road (MSR).

[1] Seibt, Sébastian (2020). "COVID-19 Creates Bumps in China's 'New Silk Road,'" *France24*, accessed 20 May 2020, available at https://www.france24.com/en/20200520-covid-19-creates-bumps-in-china-s-new-silk-road.

[2] Calabrese, John (2020). "China's Maritime Silk Road and the Middle East: Tacking against the Wind," accessed 19 May 2020, available at https://www.mei.edu/publications/chinas-maritime-silk-road-and-middle-east-tacking-against-wind.

straits: Malacca, Hormuz, Gibraltar, Suez, and Panama and these companies own stakes in about 20% of Europe's port terminals (even higher in the region around the Mediterranean such as the Port of Piraeus operated by COSCO. In just 5 years, Piraeus has gone from being a small port to the main port in the region, handling in excess of five million containers.[3]

The unexpected global pandemic prompted Chinese ironclad ally like Pakistan officially asking China in mid-April 2020 for a review of the terms and conditions of repayment of more than 100 million US dollars due in May 2020 and Beijing on 17 May 2020 agreed to extend its efforts for their "Pakistani friend" as a goodwill gesture.[4] Beijing is balancing between recouping the principal sum as well as helping with renegotiations of certain terms struck under the BRI. An anonymous researcher at the China Development Bank policy bank that manages several BRI project loans told the *Financial Times*: "We understand a lot of countries are looking to renegotiate the terms of these loans; it is a process that will take time … But it takes time to strike a new deal and we cannot even travel abroad right now. The BRI loans are not foreign aid. We need to at least recoup principal and a moderate interest."[5]

Many requests for the BRI's terms and conditionality reviews were made by African countries that are economically vulnerable to the pandemic (which China herself is also managing) and so Beijing has been working toward solutions that can show goodwill on the global stage and/or absorb costs through repayment postponements and/or debt relief.[6] China needed to show the world that it was in the BRI for the long haul. After all, the People's Republic of China (PRC) has amended its constitution to include BRI promotion which is expected to endure in the constitution until 2049 (the centennial of constitution).[7] Despite the challenges, China is trying its best to reach an equilibrium between propping up its own economy in the pandemic era (China was the only major economy that grew in 2020) and allocating budget to deal with the pandemic

---

[3] Torrent, Jordi (2020). "The New Silk Road: What Next after COVID-19?" *PierNext*, accessed 6 April 2020, available at https://piernext.portdebarcelona.cat/en/mobility/the-new-silk-road-what-next-after-covid-19/.

[4] Seibt, Sébastian (2020), *Op. cit.*

[5] *Ibid.*

[6] *Ibid.*

[7] Torrent, Jordi (2020), *Op. cit.*

economic fallout on its BRI partners (the "Silk Road friends").[8] Beijing needed to show that it can walk the talk when it came to its "Silk Road friends" in order to convince existing BRI members who overcame challenges to join the regional scheme to not regret in doing so. Sometimes such actions are reciprocal in nature. Saudi, Emirati, and Qatari officials donated medical supplies to aid China fight the virus and Middle Eastern outbreaks prompted the Chinese to send medics and medical equipment back to them (maintaining the image of dependability), placing China in a good state to have an early dip into the region's digital and healthcare infrastructure investments.[9]

The West often cited asset seizure of Sri Lanka's Hambantota Port as a warning to applicants for the BRI funding and a textbook criticism of the initiative.[10] Dissuasion was often used in persuading traditional Western allies from joining the BRI to mixed success. For example, despite intense debates on Italian membership in the BRI in early 2019 which the United States and some European institutions opposed, Italy joined alongside several Eastern European countries and some of the Chinese investments went into the establishment and management of national port and logistical infrastructure projects.[11] Other European nations appear to be staunch supporters and praise the BRI initiatives. Chief Justice Supreme Court of Russia Vyacheslav Mikhailovich Lebedev hailed the BRI-related Maritime Silk Road International Forum on Judicial Cooperation for promoting global maritime relations: "The forum will play an important role in international maritime judicial cooperation … [Russia's legislation on maritime issues will be covering all disputes and cases mentioned at the forum, including civil, penal, and administrative ones]."[12]

---

[8] Seibt, Sébastian (2020), *Op. cit.*

[9] Calabrese, John (2020), *Op. cit.*

[10] *Ibid.*

[11] Torrent, Jordi (2020), *Op. cit.*

[12] Tang, Bo (2021). "Participants Urge Seafarers' Rights Protection Amid Pandemic at the Maritime Silk Road International Forum," *CGTN*, accessed 28 October 2021, available at https://news.cgtn.com/news/2021-10-28/Forum-participants-urge-protection-of-seafarers-rights-amid-pandemic-14IXTSVWHFC/index.html.

COVID-19 Coronavirus Pandemic's Impact on the Maritime Trade Routes

Despite the COVID-19 coronavirus pandemic, China appears to trudge ahead with its plans to develop the MSR component of the BRI. In March 2020, a new container liner route was established from North China's Tianjin Municipality to Vietnam's Ho Chi Minh City, the inaugural route along the 21st Century MSR operated by the Tianjin Port Group in 2020 adding on to the 130 existing container shipping routes.[13] Tianjin Port' 32 container liner routes to Southeast Asia and hundreds of outlets in hinterland China ensure an integrated sea-rail approach for transportation of goods efficiently.[14] The importance of global ports keeping the supply chains open was highlighted in the BRI forums. For example, in the Maritime Silk Road International Forum on Judicial Cooperation, Director of legal affairs and external relations division of the International Maritime Organization Frederick Kenney highlighted the significance of shipping for the global economy.[15] To mitigate COVID-19-induced supply chain disruptions, Tianjin Port Group is working hard to sustain pandemic-era effective logistics of goods from the port to revive logistical work and manufacturing processes for a seamless operation in the global industrial and supply chain.[16]

Other than the logistical bottlenecks, some countries who participated in China's "New Silk Road" were also confronted with economic and financial issues sparked off by the unexpected pandemic situation. Critics of BRI in India, Pakistan, and some European countries have raised the loss of management control of strategic assets to Chinese entities with strategic rival the United States lobbying some states not to enter into the BRI formally or informally.[17] To placate such criticisms, China was extending an assisting hand to those affected countries while

[13] Lancang–Mekong Cooperation China Secretariat (2020). "Tianjin Port Opens New Container Route to Vietnam," *Lancang–Mekong Cooperation China (LMCCHINA)*, accessed 25 March 2020, available at http://www.lmcchina.org/eng/2020-03/25/content_41450309.html.

[14] *Ibid.*

[15] Tang, Bo (2021), *Op. cit.*

[16] Lancang-Mekong Cooperation China Secretariat (2020), *Op. cit.*

[17] Torrent, Jordi (2020), *Op. cit.*

fending off challenges to its own economy. Due to the pandemic, a growing number of economies are facing difficulties repaying the debts incurred in the silk road projects and China is working hard to prevent any debt default dangers with the countries concerned.[18] On 15 April 2020, China joined G20 members in suspending official debt service payments for the world's Least Developed Countries (LDCs) through the end of 2020.[19]

For oil-rich states, repayment for large joint venture (JV) projects is not as big an issue and they are not in economic distress.[20] For example, UAE Khalifa Port Abu Dhabi Terminal (JV between COSCO Shipping and Abu Dhabi Ports), KIZAD Logistics Park hosting 20 Chinese firms, and Abu Dhabi Port's 5,000 residential units for management/operational personnel (50-year agreement with Jiangsu Provincial Overseas Co-operation Investment Company JOCIC).[21] Besides economic and financial issues, exchanges between legal jurisdictions is also important as China, North Korea, and Hong Kong are sustaining a zero tolerance COVID-19 policy while other states are looking at COVID-resilient or co-existing with COVID-19 policies. Thus, these two systems need to be able to coordinate and talk to each other legally and judicially to resolve their differential features. At the same time, vaccinations are important factors indeed in ensuring seafarers and sailors can function normally in their jobs to maintain the global supply chain.

Southeast Asia: Cambodia

The situation of COVID-19 challenges can also be found for some countries in Southeast Asia. Cambodia for example has been indicating that BRI projects are buffering against the economic impact of COVID-19 and helping to sustain its economic development.[22] Cambodian government

---

[18] Seibt, Sébastian (2020), *Op. cit.*

[19] Calabrese, John (2020), *Op. cit.*

[20] *Ibid.*

[21] *Ibid.*

[22] Xinhua (2021). "BRI Projects Help Cambodia Cushion Economic Fallout of COVID-19 Pandemic," *Xinhuanet* edited by Huaxia, accessed 2 September 2021, available at http://www.news.cn/english/2021-09/02/c_1310163185.htm.

chief spokesman Phay Siphan said BRI projects like the Sihanoukville Special Economic Zone (SSEZ) provided benefits and economic development during the pandemic: "The SSEZ has importantly contributed to supporting the country's exports, and all hydropower plants have supplied stable electricity, which is crucial to ensure the normalcy of people's daily lives and businesses."[23]

Director of Cambodia 21st Century Maritime Silk Road Research Center Neak Chandarith noted BRI projects stabilized Cambodian economic development despite disruptions in other countries, noting "according to an operator's report, the SSEZ saw a rise of 44.51% year-on-year in the value of imports and exports reaching 1.185 billion US dollars in the first seven months of 2021."[24] Director-General of the International Relations Institute at the Royal Academy of Cambodia Kin Phea stated that the development of infrastructure such as seaports, special economic, or industrial zones under BRI can lessen logistics cost, augmenting economic competitiveness, and expanding into other sources of economic growth: "BRI also strengthens the economic performance of Cambodia. During and post-COVID-19, BRI projects will play more important role in Cambodia's economic development."[25]

The 2021 Silk Road Maritime International Cooperation Forum (under the 21st China International Fair for Investment and Trade or CIFIT) held on 8 September 2021 in Xiamen Fujian province was organized by the Fujian Provincial People's Government and the China Institute of Navigation. The Forum encouraged connectivity, port and shipping cooperation for the 21st Century MSR with the inauguration of the eighth batch of silk road shipping routes tapping into six Chinese ports: Guangzhou port, Qingdao port, Tianjin port, Xiamen port, Qinzhou port, and Fuzhou port.[26] During the pandemic, the BRI MSR appeared to sustain informational exchanges through organization of events and forum. In another Forum in October 2021, observing the seafarers/sailors'

---

[23] *Ibid.*

[24] *Ibid.*

[25] *Ibid.*

[26] Department of Commerce of Fujian Province Fujian International Investment Promotion Center CIFIT Official Website (2021). "Maritime Silk Road Exchanges Expanded at 21st CIFIT," Department of Commerce of Fujian Province Fujian International Investment Promotion Center Invest Fujian China website, accessed 12 September 2021, available at https://fdi.swt.fujian.gov.cn/en/show-11724.html.

rights of seafarers was a major discussion at the Maritime Silk Road International Forum on Judicial Cooperation held in Quanzhou Fujian Province, especially for the maritime regions of China, Southeast Asia, and the Indian subcontinent.[27]

With 80 silk road shipping routes linking 99 ports in 27 countries, the Forum's Silk Road Maritime Alliance event reached out to six new members into the umbrella of more than 210 members and they are PSA International, Guangzhou Port Group, China Railway Container Transport Corp, Dalian Maritime University, New Land-Sea Corridor Operation Co, and Huayuan International Land Port.[28] Tan Chong Meng, CEO of PSA International noted that COVID-19 has had an unprecedented impact on the world and the Silk Road Maritime Alliance will promote connectivity of the global supply chain and global trade between China, ASEAN, the United States, and Europe.[29] In fact, in promoting connectivity, the BRI also tried to organize some events to protect the individual seafarers in these extraordinary circumstances as well. Discussants from 21 countries and three International Organizations (IOs) exchanged opinions at the Maritime Silk Road International Forum on Judicial Cooperation on better protection for seafarers/sailors in shipping disputes especially during the period of the COVID-19 coronavirus pandemic.[30]

The Gulf States on the MSR

The Middle East and North African (MENA) region is a strategic crossjunction of Europe, Africa, and Asia that the BRI is connecting for a special reason which is feeding the Chinese economy with crude oil resource and, increasingly, Middle Eastern countries have also become growing consumer and infrastructure markets for Chinese contractors and trade transits onward to Europe and Africa.[31] Strategically located on the MSR, the Gulf states were some of BRI's pioneering members and a major attractor/regional hub of Chinese investments by state-owned

[27] Tang, Bo (2021), *Op. cit.*

[28] Department of Commerce of Fujian Province Fujian International Investment Promotion Center CIFIT Official Website (2021), *Op. cit.*

[29] *Ibid.*

[30] Tang, Bo (2021), *Op. cit.*

[31] Calabrese, John (2020), *Op. cit.*

enterprises (SOEs) and multinational corporations (MNCs) from the start of a comprehensive strategic partnership in 2018.[32] The initial impacts of the pandemic like rapidly falling crude oil prices, global public crisis and economic decline caused by the COVID-19 coronavirus pandemic delayed BRI projects in the region but China did not forgo the efforts to push the MSR to the Middle East and its enthusiastic regional partners at the beginning of the declaration of the pandemic.[33]

In fact, the COVID-19 coronavirus pandemic has created new cooperation potential between China and the Gulf states (including the health sector) as part of China's objective to become a "responsible great power."[34] After China contained the COVID-19 coronavirus pandemic in its own territory, the central and local authorities reacted to the MENA states by dispensing medical products and human resource to the MENA region with its state agencies, firms, and individuals providing medical advisories and scientific data to the welcoming Gulf states.[35] The focus on a health diplomacy is a two-pronged strategy that is an extension of port and industrial park construction as well. Beijing wants to integrate the Middle East into the MSR by building hybrid port-industrial park complexes connecting China to the Gulf, Arabian Sea, Red Sea, and the Mediterranean Basin and the countries in these regions have reciprocated by integrating such plans in their "national visions."[36]

Since October 2020 to May 2021, an LSE study based on 537 responses to a survey of individuals from the UAE, Saudi, Kuwait, Bahrain, Egypt, Iraq, Algeria, Jordan, Lebanon, Syria, Morocco, Tunisia, Yemen, Sudan, and Palestine indicated that 62.19% thought Arab countries should collaborate with China to fight COVID-19.[37] Vaccine availability was often a priority topic in BRI Forums which MENA economies participated. Frederick Kenney, Director of legal affairs and external relations

---

[32] Wang, Yuting and Lena Khalifa (2021). "Arab Perceptions of China During the COVID-19 Pandemic: Insights from the UAE," The London School of Economics and Political Science LSE, accessed 19 May 2021, available at https://blogs.lse.ac.uk/mec/2021/05/19/arab-perceptions-of-china-during-the-covid-19-pandemic-insights-from-the-uae/.

[33] Calabrese, John (2020), *Op. cit.*

[34] Wang, Yuting and Lena Khalifa (2021), *Op. cit.*

[35] *Ibid.*

[36] Calabrese, John (2020), *Op. cit.*

[37] Wang, Yuting and Lena Khalifa (2021), *Op. cit.*

division of the International Maritime Organization also emphasized in the Maritime Silk Road International Forum on Judicial Cooperation the availability of healthcare and vaccinations for seafarers/sailors, including repatriated personnel for priority importance to obtain vaccinations and designation as frontline key workers.[38]

Nearly 80% perceived China had a positive contribution to MENA and Chinese vaccines were a "timely roll-out of the free vaccination programme in the UAE," thus the Health Silk Road initiative's investments may be used to augment its image in the region, even though many Arabs in the UAE already perceive China as a great power and an important partner.[39] The vaccine diplomacy came on top of China's existing industrial and port infrastructure economic diplomatic initiatives. Oman, Saudi Arabia, and the United Arab Emirates (UAE) were pioneering BRI members building port-industrial park complexes connecting MENA consumer markets as three of the five ranking recipients of Chinese investments, in addition to Iraq and Algeria and their sizable domestic markets, hydrocarbon resources, and maritime access.[40] Maintenance of the BRI projects in the pandemic years fit long-term plans for the MENA states and their national agendas. The Gulf States, especially Saudi Arabia and the UAE, are keen to tap into the MSR to expand their influence in East Africa and their cooperation appear to converge with favorable public perceptions of China and compatibility between Chinese SOEs and equally state-centered Gulf power elites.[41]

MSR vs. The Overland Silk Road

Interestingly, some trade sources have mentioned that the COVID-19 coronavirus pandemic has enhanced the utilization of the New Silk Road and its high speed rail (HSR), especially for food (and beverage, F&B) and fashion firms, as articulated by Hugo Boss fashion house: "The pressure on the time to market means that we need faster modalities."[42]

[38] Tang, Bo (2021), *Op. cit.*

[39] Wang, Yuting and Lena Khalifa (2021), *Op. cit.*

[40] Calabrese, John (2020), *Op. cit.*

[41] *Ibid.*

[42] Lindert, Marcel Te, "COVID-19 Provides Boost for New Silk Road," *Supply Chain Movement (SCM) Digital Magazine*, accessed 20 November 2020, available at https://www.supplychainmovement.com/covid-19-provides-boost-for-new-silk-road/.

Shippers from the automotive, mechanical engineering, and electronics industries have become the most prolific users of the rail connections and the coronavirus pandemic has indicated the vulnerabilities of these global supply chains but the virtues appear to stand out, as mentioned by Transport Specialist Cristiano Vecci of Hugo Boss is satisfied: "Rail is a safe, fast, reliable and sustainable solution. Reliability is particularly important for us, because a week's delay can have a major impact on sales."[43] Hugo Boss Transport Specialist Cristiano Vecci also articulated: "Consumers are increasingly considering sustainability when buying clothes, and leading brands like Hugo Boss have to respond to this. In addition, new trends are coming and going increasingly rapidly, driven by social media and influencers. In order to improve our time to market, we have to look for modalities that are faster than ocean freight."[44]

Even though land transport in the overland Silk Road is speeding up logistics in the pandemic era and offers a safe/reliable option for shipping products, MSR and its logistical facilitation of products and services are not going to become irrelevant. It is not possible that rail could displace maritime logistics for moving bulk cargo due to its smaller carrying capacity and operational limitations, resulting in the cost of transporting a container by train between China and Europe two or three times more than sea freight.[45] There are some limitations to shipping products and goods by the overland route. For example, Hugo Boss ships some of its products in reefer containers.

In addition, sub-zero temperatures in Kazakhstan and Siberia may affect the quality of some textile products, as Vecci indicated: "We were afraid that the colours and quality of things like mother-of-pearl buttons on shirts would not be able to withstand the low temperatures, but after a few tests that turned out not to be an issue. So we've stopped using reefer containers for those products."[46] Another potential worries by shippers is the intensity of vibrations/movements on the actual overland journey. Hugo Boss's Vecci is anxious about knocks, bumps, and vibration during rail transport: "But we've solved that problem by packing the shoes in a different, shockproof way … For us, rail has become a stable modality

---

[43] *Ibid.*

[44] *Ibid.*

[45] Torrent, Jordi (2020), *Op. cit.*

[46] Lindert, Marcel Te, *Op. cit.*

with a lot of added value for our supply chain, and we hope to continue using it."[47]

Some solutions have facilitated overland transportation, more improvements need to be made. While Russia unbanned the transportation of agricultural products through its lands allowing the transportation of fresh produce from Europe to China, Sales Manager Will Verhees from KLG explained that some obstacles remain: "But that doesn't mean that there are no more obstacles at all. In particular, all the paperwork is still very time consuming. The customs authorities take a very outdated approach. That can be done faster and better."[48] Similarly, while the shortfall of reefer containers has been resolved with higher production, refrigeration units that come with 800-liter diesel tanks still need to be topped up using special diesel that do not gel in cold conditions.[49]

Finally, the MSR faced some challenges of its own as well. For example, the protection of the rights and interests of seafaring crew members under COVID-19 coronavirus pandemic conditions and personnel trapped on maritime vessels in quarantine for health safety concerns are some of these challenges that need multilateral judicial cooperation.[50] There are therefore incentives for seafaring nations to cooperate with one another. This is especially the case for China. Beijing has much at stakes to ensure the success of the project for the ultimate date of completion in 2049, the centenary anniversary of the founding of the PRC where the BRI is the centerpiece[51] and President Xi Jinping's most important economic diplomatic project. BRI success can enhance the Chinese Communist Party's (CCP) legitimacy and also propel Xi's personal legacy into the history books, a feature that has been very important for all rulers of China since the dynastic past.

---

[47] *Ibid.*

[48] *Ibid.*

[49] *Ibid.*

[50] Tang, Bo (2021), *Op. cit.*

[51] Calabrese, John (2020), *Op. cit.*

https://doi.org/10.1142/9789811253737_0011

Chapter 11

Omicron and Its Impact on the Modern Maritime Trading Route*

Tai Wei Lim

Introduction

In the immediate pre-coronavirus decade, shipping cargo in containers was so affordable that the industry with its excess capacity either tried to keep afloat or were bankrupted, compelling the highest-ranking shipping lines to form 3 alliances and co-use space on their sips and today, the globe's ranking 9 carriers control 83% of tonnage.[1] Ironically, such alliances and consolidation, lack of pre-pandemic investments in new vessels, and the climate change movement with stricter emission rules has possibly led to higher shipping rates and inflation.[2] With regard to inflation, a November 2021 UN report projecting a 1.5% increase in global inflation due to shipping rates, especially for lower-value products like furniture and high-tech goods with many components needed to make oceanic journeys although other argue shipping costs is still a small fraction of consumer prices.[3]

---

*Drawn from a small section of the author's writing on the Maritime Silk Road.

[1] Dempsey, Harry (2020). "Is There an End in Sight to Supply Chain Disruption?" *Financial Review*, available at https://www.afr.com/world/europe/is-there-an-end-in-sight-to-supply-chain-disruption-20220110-p59n0z.

[2] *Ibid.*

[3] *Ibid.*

Other problems that require the intervention of international organizations (IOs) like the United Nations (UN) and World Health Organization (WHO) include the international recognition of vaccines. The lack of a global vaccine standard/benchmark and different benchmarks for vaccine validity periods, caused many states to de-recognize some common WHO-approved vaccines.[4] There were also fears that Omicron could lead to less oil demand, particularly in the early days with uncertainties over its infectiousness and also severity.[5] While oil prices are more market-oriented and there is a limit to how much governments can intervene in those prices, IOs can work more effectively with national governments in the arena of vaccination programs. Seafarer vaccination rates are at 59.8%, compared to the equivalent of the percentage of general population (the EU at 68%, Hong Kong's 63%, Japanese rate at 79%, Singapore's 83%, the UK's 71% and United States at 62%).[6] The gap between seafarer and general population's vaccination rates can be closed further.

Approximately 90% of global trade takes place in the maritime trading routes, thus the COVID-19 coronavirus pandemic has affected all shipping ecosystem entities equally, including the producers ranging from Argentinian wineries needed to ship their products overseas to Sri Lankan clothing manufacturers meeting export orders.[7] Given that it is a global crisis, it is also an incentive for countries to cooperate to roll out vaccination programs. International Seafarer vaccinations are moving alongside general vaccine programs in many countries,[8] given that it is not just the port bottlenecks and crowded go-downs but also the ships at sea that have experienced delays which led to a global semiconductor shortage and petrochemical unavailability.[9] In addition, seafarers' vaccination rates even in the most advanced countries fell behind their general population's vaccination rates. The January 2022 Indicator revealed that the aggregate

[4] The Editorial Team (2022). "Crew Change Crisis Getting Better, But Omicron Variant Poses New Difficulties," *Safety4Sea/Seafarers*, accessed 13 January 2022, available at https://safety4sea.com/crew-change-crisis-getting-better-but-omicron-variant-poses-new-difficulties/.

[5] Dempsey, Harry (2020), *Op. cit.*

[6] The Editorial Team (2022), *Op. cit.*

[7] Dempsey, Harry (2020), *Op. cit.*

[8] The Editorial Team (2022), *Op. cit.*

[9] Dempsey, Harry (2020), *Op. cit.*

percentage of vaccinated seafarers from the sample increased from 49.5% in December 2021 to 59.8% in January 2020, compared to the general population of fully vaccinated individuals in several major European/North American/Asian shipping nations hovering at or above 70%.[10] The pandemic has disrupted a meticulously choreographed balance between production and logistics as pandemic-era container shipping had to cope an accelerated consumer demand for goods which coincided with reduction of manufacturing capacity in the early lockdowns in the first half of 2020.[11]

The logistical bottlenecks resulted in expensive freight costs, restricted cargo space on ships, empty store shelves for consumers, less product access for consumers, chronic delivery delays, increasing consumer prices, rise of inflation, and supply chain disruptions.[12] China is a major factor in the supply chain disruptions as the "world's factory." After the Omicron outbreak, China strengthened its "zero-COVID" policy which used to involve city-wide mass lockdowns, compulsory quarantines, and strict port controls to track ships and cargoes in an attempt to stop new infections, a policy that has grave consequences for the global logistical industry as China is home to 7 of the 10 biggest container ports (including Shanghai).[13] Terminal closures in 2021 at two of the world's five busiest container ports (Shenzhen and Ningbo-Zhoushan in China) after COVID-19 outbreaks and blockage of the Suez Canal by a 400-meter-long vessel, added to global delivery delays.[14] Vice-Chairperson of global logistics operations at Taiwanese Wan Hai Lines Randy Chen opined that it has been an uphill climb for COVID-19-affected ports, warehouses, and trucking to return back to normal.[15]

The onset of Omicron infection came suddenly and without prior warning of its arrival. It caused great fear to shippers and logistics industry and

---

[10] The Editorial Team (2022), *Op. cit.*

[11] Dempsey, Harry (2020), *Op. cit.*

[12] *Ibid.*

[13] Zeymarine (2022). "New COVID-19 Omicron Effects on Shipping Industry," accessed 10 January 2022, available at https://zeymarine.com/new-covid-19-omicron-effects-on-shipping-industry/#:~:text=The%20spread%20of%20the%20Omicron,continue%20or%20revive%20with%202022.&text=As%20a%20result%2C%20problems%20in%20the%20supply%20chain%20may%20persist.

[14] Dempsey, Harry (2020), *Op. cit.*

[15] *Ibid.*

many scrambled in the early days of Omicron, trying to cope with further disruptions as the world waited for data from South Africa to come in with regard to its severity. The anxiety was well understood by the logistical and shipping industry because their shipments had already been delayed even before the onset of Omicron. Many countries had their hands full dealing with the Delta infections. There are were also intelligence of some Russian and Eastern European reluctance toward vaccination, affecting regional crew supply and crew-changes.[16] By 10 January 2022, only 25% of mariners/sailors were vaccinated, becoming an obstacle to sea voyages, in addition to limiting crew retention and mobility on board ships while seafarers refusing to return to ships are also increasing as they become attracted to the higher salaries of other sub-sectors of the transportation industry.[17] The Neptune Declaration Crew Change Indicator for January 2022 indicated that seafarers on ships staying beyond contract expiration has dropped from 4.7% to 3.7% in December 2020 but that news was mitigated by the simultaneous emergence of the Omicron coronavirus.[18]

The Impact on Small and Medium-Sized Enterprises (SMEs)

The impact of the pandemic extended to the most vulnerable sector of the private enterprise. Times were also especially tough for SMEs. Smaller firms have had to compete aggressively to get more container space on ships to export goods in order to maintain their manufacturing and shore up sales activities to stave off cash flow pressure, deplete their backlog and cope with rising freight rates (7 times on average compared to pre-pandemic levels).[19] Some businesses are now affected having to dish out much higher payments. It comes up approximately 15,000 US dollars ($20,880) to transport a 40-foot container from China to the American west coast, which is 10 times more than the pre-pandemic market rate and may go even higher due to the higher spot market rates locked into annual freight contracts and rumor/fear-mongering over disruptions utilized as a bargaining tools by the carriers.[20] This also applies to smaller economies

---

[16] The Editorial Team (2022), *Op. cit.*

[17] Zeymarine (2022), *Op. cit.*

[18] The Editorial Team (2022), *Op. cit.*

[19] Dempsey, Harry (2020), *Op. cit.*

[20] *Ibid.*

as well. Sean van Dort, Logistics Chairman of the trade body Joint Apparel Association Forum Sri Lanka, noted that fewer ships are now stopping at Colombo to offload East Asian fabrics, yarns, and accessories required by garment suppliers to multinational brand producers:

> Many small and medium-sized companies have had to close or temporarily shut down as they don't have the financial power to air freight goods … [Shipping lines are] a moth to the flame and go where the higher freight rates are.[21]

The Impact of Festivals and Holidays

There were numerous personal stories of how logistical players feared the onset of Omicron, especially since it triggered off pre-Christmas lockdowns. For example, Bob Biesterfeld, the person in charge of CH Robinson, North America's biggest freight broker, was still working with his haulier staff members offloading severely delayed Halloween costumes (of vampires, ghosts, and witches) from freight boxes at the LA and Long Beach port storage areas due to the disruptions caused to maritime logistics during the COVID-19 coronavirus pandemic.[22] Cargoes were stacked up and remained immobile in the Los Angeles port due to delays in all sections of the logistical/transportation delivery systems. This is the case not only in the US but also in Europe, pre-Christmas lockdowns, and more restrictions on mobility in other countries have affected the confidence in the global logistical system to deliver on time.[23] Johanna Urkauf, Managing Director of Austrian KTM Bike Industries bicycle maker noted: "Our warehouse is full, but there are always one or two parts missing."[24]

Besides festivals and holidays in the US adding to the logistical pressure, there are similar causes on the East Asian side as well. Annual festivals and their festivities like the Chinese New Year (CNY also known as the Lunar New Year, Tet for the Vietnamese) has resulted in a spike in container shipping, eased only slightly industrial factories' closures due to the holidays, a trend also noted by Chief Executive of DHL Express John

---

[21] *Ibid.*

[22] *Ibid.*

[23] Zeymarine (2022), *Op. cit.*

[24] Dempsey, Harry (2020), *Op. cit.*

Pearson.[25] The crunch for more products and goods will arrive after the Lunar New Year due to the need to replenish used-up inventories that have been depleted to historical low levels and this could accentuate in the peak container shipping summer season to be in time for the Black Friday and Christmas 2022 goods/products.[26] Besides the Lunar New Year, Ron Widdows, a former shipping executive and chief of FlexiVan (one of North America's biggest fleets of chassis-steel frames attached to lorry cabs and carry containers) said is prepared for more slowdown in some Chinese manufacturing activities during the Winter Olympics in Beijing when strict COVID-19 coronavirus quarantine rules are in place for sailors.[27]

Speedy Instant Reactions to Omicron

Omicron immediately triggered many governments to review their COVID-19 coronavirus protocols and reintroduce restrictions that impeded crew-change on the ships.[28] In the early days of the Omicron emergence, some countries suspended crew change and vaccination of those sailors with recent travels to Botswana, Eswatini, Lesotho, Mozambique, Namibia, South Africa, and Zimbabwe within two weeks of arriving at the port (approximately at least 56 countries came up with travel limitations due to Omicron).[29] China hosts 7 of the ranking 10 global container ports (including number one Shanghai) and has imposed the zero COVID policy, resulting in the Xian lockdown of 13 million people in December 2021; Hong Kong ban on passenger flights from 8 countries (including the US) and a partial shutdown of Ningbo was partially shut down in January 2022.[30] The disadvantage of speedy lockdowns and travel restrictions is what some industry players label as "knee-jerk" reactions that cut off supply chains or even cause them to break down as Willie Walsh, Director General IATA said in MarPro:

---

[25] *Ibid.*

[26] *Ibid.*

[27] *Ibid.*

[28] The Editorial Team (2022), *Op. cit.*

[29] Transport Capital (2022). "How Will Omicron Affect the Maritime & Aviation Industries?" accessed 1 February 2022, available at https://transportcapital.com/will-omicron-affect-the-maritime-aviation-industries/.

[30] Dempsey, Harry (2020), *Op. cit.*

"After nearly two years of dealing with COVID-19, we should have progressed beyond these knee-jerk, uncoordinated, Pavlovian-like responses."[31]

When the infections in parts of Europe and North American surged ahead of South Africa, the meticulous scientific data collected from these two regions of the world really helped with understanding Omicron in a much better way. The transparency of such data released helped to put the world at ease in the intermediate stages of Omicron infections. Some world regions are not waiting for the full set of data to come out before implementing coping mechanisms to correct trade imbalance and global shipping trends. Europe is one such example. Shipping firms' stops at the five largest Asian and northern European ports on weekly loops dropped by 25% since 2016 and even faster during the pandemic (Alphaliner consultancy data), prompting the Europeans to react in the manner articulated by Lars Mikael Jensen, Head of Global Ocean Network at Maersk:

> [referring to a shift to the "more hub-and-spoke" model adopted by the Danish shipping conglomerate] Instead of calling at every port directly, we put [the cargo] on to feeders at a connection point … That will make the network less dependent on individual delays at ports... this is something we're looking to do more of."[32]

Yet, another view is that Omicron's impact on immobility may encourage consumers to spend more given that they are unable to travel free and this could benefit goods over services and help container shipping rates as Clarksons Platou Securities commented in *Freight Waves*' report:

> With omicron now causing more restrictive travel measures, consumer spending habits may remain engaged in the favour of the container shipping sector. Several liners had already taken a view that strong market

[31] Transport Capital (2022), *Op. cit*.

[32] Dempsey, Harry, "Is there an end in sight to supply chain disruption?" dated 10 January 2022 in Financial Review [downloaded on 10 January 2022], available at https://www.afr.com/world/europe/is-there-an-end-in-sight-to-supply-chain-disruption-20220110-p59n0z.

> conditions will persist into 2022, and this could be extended further … [with] a potentially longer run."[33]

Chief Executive of the Global Shippers Forum trade group representing importers and exporters James Hookham argues, as Omicron ebbs and subsides, tourism, hospitality, and other services alongside higher prices/interest rates for goods may ease:

> I'm not buying the hype that says we will endure this for most of 2022 ... There's no inevitably about the continuing high levels of demand for container shipping.[34]

On the flip-side, if consumer goods demand stay strong, industry watchers opine that it will be hard to settle the existing backlog of goods. This is because US consumers typically allocate 60% of spending to goods and 40% to services but this has increased to 65% for goods during the pandemic, resulting in 20% increase in US imports in September/October 2021 over the same period in 2019.[35]

Concluding Remarks

The causes for the shipping bottlenecks and their impacts on the global economy are complex. There are many explanations for it, only some will be highlighted here. President of UPS International Scott Price regard the pandemic as a "migration to new supply chain models" as firms/industries shift complex goods manufacturing sites nearer to their consumer markets to fight higher transport costs and the end of affordable Chinese labor costs.[36] Another cause may be the decisions of shippers to focus more ships on profitable shipping lanes like those between North America and Asia which expanded by 30% between January–December 2021 (Alphaliner consultancy data) while those catering to Africa and between

[33] Transport Capital, "How Will Omicron Affect the Maritime & Aviation Industries?" in Transport Capital website [downloaded on 1 February 2022], available at https://transportcapital.com/will-omicron-affect-the-maritime-aviation-industries/.

[34] Dempsey, Harry, *Op. cit.*

[35] *Ibid.*

[36] *Ibid.*

Asian nations decreased 3.3% and 10%, respectively, in the same period.[37] As COVID-19 coronavirus mutates, Omicron is just one of thousands of mutations and more variants will appear likely emerge in the future, and state behavior as well as consumer reactions to these variants will continue to shape the maritime shipping industry. The industry players along with officials needed to calibrate their policies and actions carefully to prevent any crew-change crisis and reversing progress made in restoring global trade and supply chains and to work together to ensure that the impact of crew changes due to Omicron is reduced.

[37] *Ibid.*

https://doi.org/10.1142/9789811253737_0012

Chapter 12

Last Word: Globalization, De-globalization, and Anti-globalization

Wing Lok Hung

When historian Niall Ferguson wrote the article "Sinking Globalization" in the *Foreign Affairs* in 2005, we were reminded of when the global economy was astonishingly disintegrated throughout horrendous periods during World War I, the Great Depression, and the Second World War.[1] However, perhaps only very few people would have imagined that our golden age of globalization would rapidly be obstructed in a similar way to what our grandparents' experienced when WWII broke out and the Cold War that followed. The disintegration of our modern globalized world due to a worldwide spread of an infectious disease would also have been unimaginable.

The COVID-19 pandemic is certainly a tipping point for globalization in the 21st century and invites comparison to a global phenomenon that defined the early 20th century: de-globalization. If "globalization" is generally defined as the flow of global trade, goods and services, and free movement of labor and activity of multinational corporations, "de-globalization" is simply the opposite. In short, de-globalization can be described as a

[1] Ferguson, Niall (2005). "Sinking Globalization," *Foreign Affairs*, 84(2), 64–77.

tendency toward a less connected world.[2] Historically, great-power conflicts contributed to the process of de-globalization in several periods before 1945. The world opted to close economic borders and reduce the flow of global goods and labor. The setbacks of globalization have been subtly different during the COVID-19 pandemic. National borders were closed mainly due to each government's strict quarantine measures to prevent the spread of infectious disease. In America, protective equipment such as non-medical masks and respirators were blocked for sale overseas to fulfil domestic needs.[3] Cross-border logistics and supply chains have also been a problem. For example, thousands of UK petrol stations were closed due to the shortage of truck drivers.[4] Hong Kong's fresh food and vegetables supplies were sporadically disrupted in the surging fifth wave of COVID-19 in February 2022 (see Figure 1).[5] There were various factors behind each issue including an aging workforce, Britain's departure from the European Union, and unattractive job prospects in several local industries. It was simply a perfect storm exacerbated by the COVID-19.

The Fate of Global Cities in a De-globalized World

This has led to an important question related to globalization in a post-COVID world. Can a highly globalized city survive in a de-globalized world? Unlike many other places in the world, Hong Kong lacks a sufficient local food supply and agricultural products. Free market capitalism did not work as people were restricted in the amount of packaged

---

[2] Markus Kornprobst and Jon Wallace (2021). "What is Deglobalization?" Chatham House, 18 October, available at https://www.chathamhouse.org/2021/10/what-deglobalization.

[3] "Trump Seeks to Block 3M Mask Exports and Grab Masks from Its Overseas Customers," *New York Times*, 3 April 2020, available at https://www.nytimes.com/2020/04/03/us/politics/coronavirus-trump-3m-masks.html.

[4] "Britain Scrambles for Truck Drivers as Queues Form at Petrol Stations Amid Shortage," *South China Morning Post*, 24 September 2021, available at https://www.scmp.com/news/world/europe/article/3150025/britain-scrambles-truck-drivers-queues-form-petrol-stations-amid.

[5] "Vegetable Prices in Hong Kong Continue to Rise as COVID-19 Cases among Cross-Border Truckers Force Stricter Testing Requirements," *South China Morning Post*, 7 February 2022, available at https://www.scmp.com/news/hong-kong/hong-kong-economy/article/3166152/vegetable-prices-hong-kong-continue-rise-covid-19.

vegetables they could purchase per day (see Figure 2). Innovative navigation and transportation and the growth of the middle class and capital have also not improved global interconnections during the pandemic. Before the pandemic, global interconnections often meant lower prices, higher quality, and better delivery in a free liberal market. However, timely delivery has been far more important than price and quality in a de-globalized world. People and restaurants were worried about a shortage of fresh food and other necessities due to supply delays.

Multinational corporations (MNCs) are distinctive features of global cities but the immense power of MNCs has been challenged under COVID-19. It was found that MNCs suffered a greater loss in firm value relative to domestic firms during the market crisis caused by the coronavirus.[6] Due to the severe disruption to global supply chains and global value chains, it is not surprising that the pandemic has made MNCs vulnerable to risk. Exxon Mobile, for example, which was once a top 500 Forbes Global company, recorded a historical annual loss of 22.4 billion US dollars and announced a plan to reduce its global workforce by 14,000 people in 2020.[7] There was also uncertainty in tourism and foreign investment for global cities during the pandemic and this resulted in some companies moving abroad. For example, Royal Caribbean International moved its Spectrum of the Seas vessel from Hong Kong to Singapore in early 2022.[8] In a survey, 42.9% of Japanese companies in Hong Kong had been ordered or urged by their management to consider reducing the number of employees in their Hong Kong offices.[9] With the disruption to the

---

[6] Guedhami, Omrane, April M. Knill, William L. Megginson, and Lemma W. Senbet, "The Dark Side of Globalization: Evidence from the Impact of COVID-19 on Multinational Companies," 22 June 2021, available at https://ssrn.com/abstract=3868449.

[7] "Exxon to Close Two Houston-Area Office Towers after Staff Departures," *Reuters*, 23 October 2021, available at https://www.reuters.com/business/exxon-close-two-houston-area-office-towers-after-staff-departures-2021-10-22/.

[8] "Coronavirus Hong Kong: Royal Caribbean Axes Local 'Cruises to Nowhere,' Moves Ship to Singapore over Tough Anti-Pandemic Measures," *South China Morning Post*, 9 February 2022, available at https://www.scmp.com/news/hong-kong/hong-kong-economy/article/3166344/coronavirus-hong-kong-royal-caribbean-axes-local.

[9] "在港日本企業第九回「香港營商環境」調研發布　對港府提五個訴求," HK01, 26 January 2022, available at https://www.hk01.com/%E5%8D%B3%E6%99%82%E5%9C%8B%E9%9A%9B/729092/%E5%9C%A8%E6%B8%AF%E6%97%A5%E6%9C%AC%E4%BC%81%E6%A5%AD%E7%AC%AC%E4%B9%9D%E5%9B%9E-%E9%A6%99%E6%B8%AF%E7%87%9F%E5%95%86%E7%92%B0%E5%A2%83-%E8%AA%

Figure 1. Fresh vegetables fly off the shelves at a supermarket in Hong Kong. Photo taken by the author on 13 February 2022.

global flow of goods and tourists continuing, many companies were forced to cut jobs and cut costs. A global city without a consistent flow of trade and people across borders could cause significant social and economic problems for the people in these cities.

In fact, there have always been controversies in globalization and early warning signs were found in the pre-COVID-19 world. The Brexit vote outcome in 2015 and the ongoing decoupling of the world's two largest economies have almost certainly affected the process of globalization. The consequences of COVID-19 have highlighted the importance and

BF%E7%A0%94%E7%99%BC%E5%B8%83-%E5%B0%8D%E6%B8%AF%E5%BA%9C%E6%8F%90%E4%BA%94%E5%80%8B%E8%A8%B4%E6%B1%82.

Figure 2. Restrictions on the purchase of packaged vegetables at a supermarket in Hong Kong. Photo taken by the author on 13 February 2022.

significance of retaining a domestic city rather than transforming into a global city. Otherwise, another sudden and unexpected de-globalization would create more losers than winners. The impact was more severe for global cities if they were heavily relied on foreign goods and labor. Inconveniences in modern daily life would hinder the pursuit of a better world with cosmopolitan or communitarian principles.

Rethinking Globalization and International Institutions

The COVID-19 pandemic has also exposed the weaknesses in our international cooperation system. Modern globalization has generally occurred in three major waves. The first from 1870 to 1914. The ideas of classical liberalism promoted the first wave of globalization. In short, the *laissez-faire* economy was not regulated by the state but by the "invisible hand" — an unintended consequence of a group of self-interested individuals.[10] Nevertheless, recently, the free market approach has not been

[10] Green, Jeremy (2019). *Is Globalization Over*? Polity, pp. 26–27.

Table 1. Full vaccination (at least two doses of the vaccine) rates in major Asian countries/regions.

Countries/regions	Fully vaccinated (per 100 people)	Vaccinated with at least one dose (per 100 people)
Brunei	92	92
Singapore	90	91
South Korea	86	87
Cambodia	82	85
Malaysia	79	82
Japan	79	81
Vietnam	78	81
Thailand	71	76
Hong Kong SAR	68	78
Laos	58	66
Indonesia	52	69
Myanmar	38	43

Source: https://ourworldindata.org/covid-vaccinations (Date last updated on 11 February 2022).

functioning as global customers rushed to panic-buy disposable marks, antigen test kits, or even toilet papers during the COVID-19 pandemic. The second wave of globalization was from 1945 to 2000s. This wave of globalization focused more on international financial cooperation. After the Second World War, leading European states and United States of America designed a set of international institutions, regulations, and norms to steer a new liberal economic order. Japan and the successful stories of "Asian Tigers" after the Second World War also contributed to and celebrated the golden era of globalization. With more than 50 years of regional integration, Asian countries have failed to establish a public health cooperation under globalization. There was disparity in vaccination rates in Asia, and some Southeast Asian countries did not have enough vaccines for the public while Hong Kong had a large amount of unused COVID-19 vaccine doses due to having a relatively low vaccination rate in 2021 (Table 1).[11]

[11] "Government Responds to Use of COVID-19 Vaccines," Press Releases — The Government of the Hong Kong Special Administrative Region, 25 May 2021, available at

Before the COVID-19 pandemic, experts and governments were prepared to outline a new architecture for Globalization 4.0 and its integration with the Fourth Industrial Revolution.[12] The next wave of Globalization 3.0 is to create a global digital world from the ability to innovate, robotize, and digitalize. However, the sudden devastation of global economics due to COVID-19 has set back the next wave of globalization. The lack of international consensus on the decisions made to tackle COVID-19 has also further delayed the next wave of globalization. Rich countries should have distributed vaccines to developing countries in a timely manner. But the truth was that poor countries only received nearly expired COVID-19 vaccine doses.[13] In the face of this unprecedented public health crisis, the role of intergovernmental organizations and international non-governmental organizations have so far insufficiently handled the crisis. A stable and sustainable international organization was at stake. Former US President Donald Trump has previously declared that he would like the United States to stop funding the World Health Organization.[14] Similarly, there were chaotic implementations of vaccine passports as various countries set different rules and regulations. A stable and efficient international institution is difficult to establish.

The Making of Anti-Globalization in the Post-COVID World

The devastating memories of COVID-19 have taught us an unforgettable lesson that many modern economic and social issues cannot be resolved by globalization. On the contrary, there is great reluctance to adopt a global standard in combating this resilient virus. Due to differences in

---

https://www.info.gov.hk/gia/general/202105/25/P2021052500953.htm.

[12] Schwab, Klaus (2019). "Globalization 4.0: A New Architecture for the Fourth Industrial Revolution," *Foreign Affairs*, 16 January, available at https://www.foreignaffairs.com/articles/world/2019-01-16/globalization-40.

[13] "Poorer Nations Reject over 100 mln COVID-19 Vaccine Doses as Many Near Expiry," *Reuters*, 14 January 2022. available at https://www.reuters.com/business/healthcare-pharmaceuticals/more-than-100-million-covid-19-vaccines-rejected-by-poorer-nations-dec-unicef-2022-01-13/.

[14] Tufekci, Zeynep (2020). "The WHO Shouldn't Be a Plaything for Great Powers," *The Atlantic*, 16 April 2020, available at https://www.theatlantic.com/health/archive/2020/04/why-world-health-organization-failed/610063/.

social culture and economic structures, some regions have preferred to adopt a "living with virus" approach while some have preferred a "zero-tolerance" approach to COVID-19. This disagreement was particularly obvious in the latest global developments of the COVID-19 pandemic. It confirmed a skeptic's view on globalization that the ideology of globalism is simply a myth in the face of national interests, ethnicity, social culture, and geopolitics. There are almost no standardized rules and regulations to ensure stability among modern societies during the pandemic.

By contrast, the structural inequality of market-led globalization provided more problems than solutions to developing countries. For example, African countries generally have less financial resources to purchase medicine and medical supplies during the pandemic. Global suppliers were unlikely to export medical goods to the African continent while there was a surge in demand for face masks in Europe and Asia. Transportation was another concern throughout the pandemic. For example, delivery of medical masks to most African countries from Hong Kong was suspended.[15] Nevertheless, it did not mean that fewer COVID cases were found in developing countries. Various African countries adopted lockdown measures to contain the spread of COVID-19.[16] People had to wash hands outside banks, shops, and large sports gatherings were canceled. But life went on as normal when most people were living in rural areas of African countries such as Rwanda.[17] In short, COVID-19 has created a wide range of transnational problems, from issues with global supplies to the disrupted functioning of modern societies. If globalization fails to build a better world with the ideal economic efficiency and equity, this will surely strengthen anti-globalization voices in the post-COVID world.

---

[15] Personal Experience in April 2020. See the most updated notices from *Hongkong Post*, available at https://www.hongkongpost.hk/en/about_us/whats_new/notices/index_id_1109.html.

[16] "COVID-19: Rwanda Lifts Kigali Lockdown, Strict Measures Remain," *The East African*, 2 August 2021, available at https://www.theeastafrican.co.ke/tea/news/east-africa/rwanda-lifts-kigali-lockdown-3494858.

[17] Email communications with Sabrina Joy Smith in Rwanda, 11 March 2020.

https://doi.org/10.1142/9789811253737_0013

Chapter 13

Conclusion

Tai Wei Lim

In conclusion, this volume's multidisciplinary gathering of scholars noted that there is continuity and discontinuity in COVID-19 coronavirus' impact on various case studies in this volume. For example, Godo's chapter indicated that the pandemic has compounded existing challenges by compounding existing problems and/or overturning challenges that were on the way to resolution. For example, Godo noted that, just before the outbreak of the COVID-19, the Japanese agricultural sector was showing faint but growing signs of overcoming its two long-standing problems, i.e., shrinkage of food demands and shortage of agricultural laborers. Shrinkage of food demands comes from de-population and prolonged economic stagnation since the early 1990s.

Shortage of agricultural laborers comes from the changing work ethic among Japanese laborers whereby younger generations have begun to move away from manual work such as farming. However, the recent steep surge in incoming foreign sightseers and agricultural laborers was showing a possible solution. Inbounding foreign sightseers (in particular, from rising Asian countries such as China) has been showing strong demands for Japan's high-quality (and high-price) agricultural products, such as Wagyu beef and white strawberries. By presenting new schemes for employing foreign agricultural laborers in 2017 and 2018, the Japanese government, which had been conservative in immigration policy, turned to be aggressive in inviting foreign agricultural laborers.

Godo detected how the COVID-19 outbreak brought about a reversal just when farmers' positive expectations were growing. The number of inbound foreign sightseers has dropped to a negligible level, and it has become difficult for foreign agricultural laborers to come to Japan. In addition, due to the government's requests for suspension of the business and schooling, food demands for business use and school lunch shrank. Godo then zoomed into the institutional players and noted that they too had to adapt to a world that was already changing before the pandemic and has to adapt even more to a post-pandemic world where new roles must be explored to stay relevant to the economic system. For example, Godo concludes that the electoral and financial reforms in the middle of the 1990s deprived Nokyo of these advantages. As a result, Nokyo's economic and political power declined over the past 20 years. It is no longer a key player in agricultural political dynamics. It should be noted that earlier, Nokyo's close relationship with the LDP contradicted political neutrality, which is essential in the ideology of corporatism. In that sense, it may be the time for Nokyo to return to pure corporatism.

Historically, Yokohama Chinatown had encountered other apocalyptic events. Just like coronavirus is a natural phenomenon (at the point of this writing, most scientists established that the COVID-19 coronavirus is not a lab-made pathogen), another kind of disaster in the form of a massive apocalyptic earthquake also hit the Chinatown in 1923. The year 2020 turned out to be a very challenging year for everyone. Japan and the world were struck by the COVID-19 coronavirus pandemic which caught the world by surprise starting from 23 January 2020 when it was publicly revealed by the Chinese authorities. Tourists headed for the Chinatown declined in numbers as early as January 2020 when Japan confirmed its first COVID-19 infection. This was made worse by fake news that the infected individual was from the Chinatown and, by March 2020, some eateries in the Chinatown received racially charged messages attributing the outbreak to Chinese individuals and demanded them to "get out of Japan soon" (*Kyodo News Agency/Mainichi Shimbun*, 2020). Yokohama Chinatown restaurateurs sought solidarity with other nearby premium establishments to cope with the economic impact of COVID-19 coronavirus pandemic.

In solidarity with other external retailers to drawn tourists and visitors back, Yokohama Chinatown residents and their Japanese allies and stakeholders are working together to combat a common enemy — the economic impact of the COVID-19 coronavirus pandemic which does not differentiate between retailers or the prestige of the addresses. Wong and Lee conclude that, due to the strains of repeated states of emergency, it may not be surprising to see more restaurants and shops in Yokohama Chinatown close down in near future. No one is able to tell when the "light" will finally be able to seen at the end of the tunnel. But, with the new measures and business models, cooperation within the overseas Chinese community and support from mainstream Japanese society, someday Yokohama Chinatown will be lively again.

Resilience as a theme is also found in the civil society sector as we read Ng Ka-shing's chapter on Hong Kong's Resilience in the Face of COVID-19 through examining the role of civil society amid adversity. While Hong Kong government measures are largely effective, the role of Hong Kong's civil society in fighting the outbreak cannot be ignored. For example, many companies have promptly implemented work-from-home in February; the general public immediately adopted the habit of mask-wearing despite government's face marks ban enacted in October 2019 as a means to suppress continuous mass protests. Especially, when the government was reluctant to solve the mask shortage problem initially, NGOs and individuals promptly responded by distributing free marks to the public and opening factories to manufacture masks.

These examples show that the civil society in Hong Kong has shown strong resilience in the face of virus and government's "inability" to deal with the mask crisis. The chapter explored the role of civil society in the battle with COVID-19 in Hong Kong with a particular focus on the mask shortage problem. For example, how charitable groups, religious organizations, and other NGOs responded to the mask problem and how experts and laymen, without any assistance from government, acted individually to help solve the crisis. Ng's analysis, conducted mainly through textual materials, such as news articles as well as activity reports issued by NGOs, argues the importance of civil society in the fight against COVID-19, and the findings can further contribute to the debate and literature of civil society. He concludes that the COVID-19 pandemic has accentuated both the weaknesses and strengths of many countries. In the case of Hong Kong, the civil society, which has actively engaged in promoting the betterment of society, has also shown strong resilience in responding to the crisis. It also suggests a healthy and strong civil society is vital for managing risks for every society as the authority may sometimes fail.

Kenneth Wong's excellent chapter indicates Singapore's all-of-society preparedness in dealing with the pandemic. Leading the battle against COVID-19, Singapore government and various stakeholders in the community, through the Public, Private and People approach, rallied together to address the various social, health, financial challenges that arose in the pandemic. The battle against COVID-19 pandemic is far from over and Singapore, as well as countries around the world, should never let their guard down. Many countries including Hong Kong, Australia, and Western countries are facing several waves of outbreaks, forcing the countries to go into partial/full lockdown once again, affecting their economies.

Satoshi Abe's chapter, a highlight in this volume, tackled the complex question of humankind and its relationship with science and religion. It stands out as a chapter that deals with very esoteric question, yet one that is fraught with practical consequences. In response to the spread of the disease, on the one hand, the Iranian government urgently took measures based on scientific findings, for example, by closing mosque gates throughout the city and canceling Friday congregations for quarantine purposes. On the other hand, groups of religionists protested against these government's measures by flocking themselves at the mosque gates for demanding prayers inside or by clandestinely turning to the curing techniques prescribed by Islamic medicine to contend that Islam can be a legitimate curative guide for the containment of COVID-19. The chapter examined religious debates in Iran that are increasingly gaining public attention in the midst of the coronavirus pandemic. It elucidates the rationales of the government with a particular focus on how they project the languages of Islam onto discussions concerning COVID-19, the field of which is predominately organized and defined through modern science. The textual analyzes also shed light on the styles of reasoning articulated by the religionists to help us situate their understanding of the phenomena based on their own religious viewpoints. In doing so, the present work seeks to understand the emergence and development of Islamic tradition in Iran, in which correct forms of Islam, ways of religious contributions, and roles of religion are debated for securing public hygiene.

This chapter looked at how the COVID-19 pandemic unfolded in Iran, a country in which state affairs operate under the checks of a religious establishment, and presented the kinds of activities, debates, and rationales that religious leaders engage in to confront the pandemic. From the early phase of the virus's upsurge, the Ministry of Health has been held accountable for handling public health measures, including disinfection, mask-wearing, and social distancing, and has been leading the efforts to curtail virus transmission at the national level. The Ministry of Health particularly draws upon modern science to understand the mechanism of virus transmission and to formulate public health guidelines therefrom. As a result, the field of public health is increasingly organized through a scientific paradigm, prompting religious leaders to become involved in conversations about the practical and theological implications of modern science. Abe concluded with an observation of the shifting terrain of the relationship between modern science and Islam in Iran during the COVID-19 pandemic, this relationship being contingently conditioned by the discourses and practices surrounding the field of public health to which both modern science and Islam contribute in a distinctively historical manner.[1]

Still on the theme of technology, Lim's chapter was a future-oriented one focusing on the relationship between COVID-19 and technology. In his chapter, Lim noted how countries the world over have deployed their best possible capabilities such as advanced robotics, telemedicine, tracking systems, and big data analytics in their combat against the COVID-19 epidemic. Creative predictive models to project the spread and proliferation of the virus have been made possible by the use of algorithms, Artificial Intelligence (AI), and data analytics in analyzing big data. These sophisticated systems also represent tech capabilities and strengths of countries and carry implications for the tech sector post-COVID-19. Robots now work hand in hand with human operators who program them to clean up areas and deliver meals, beverages, and pharmaceuticals to people who need them while other categories of robots collect and supply data.

To prevent infected or potentially infected patients from turning up at clinics, community hospitals and polyclinics, doctors, health planners, and other stakeholders are using technologies to remotely connect these groups with doctors and medical practitioners to treat the patients from afar. However, there are also groups and individuals who are pushing back on such technological breakthroughs. The constant tensions between tech advocates and push-back resistance are likely to continue. Finally, he noted that states are not waiting for tech sceptics to voice their complete

[1] Elshakry (2013) examines the historically contingent ways in which modern science was uniquely introduced to Islamic contexts by tracing the debates about Darwin's *The Origin of Species* in the Arab world. Elshakry, M. (2013). *Reading Darwin in Arabic, 1860–1950*. Chicago, IL: The University of Chicago Press.

support before they forge ahead with plans to create consortiums and partnerships of multiple tech systems to have a consolidated tech approach in battling the COVID-19 disease. The pandemic may stimulate many in medical establishments to change the way they practice medicine and reduce face-to-face consultations in the future, except for the most critical cases.

Ma's chapter illuminates how the COVID-19 pandemic has brought about novel legal issues, with public health concerns at the core of such issues, including the possibility of infringing or limiting the rights of citizens. The HKSAR government has striven to balance the needs of healthcare concern with the voices from the public on the infringement of citizens' rights. Private citizens were also required to reexamine and renegotiate their rights and obligations in the business and employment setting in light of the pandemic. The Hong Kong courts have ruled on various disputes between litigants on the change in legal relations because of the onset of COVID-19 pandemic. She ends on a befitting note that is perhaps appropriate for this volume's own final word: "Thanks to the release of various COVID-19 vaccines and the recent news of Pfizer's antiviral treatment … have reduced the death rate and hospitalization by 89%, it is hoped that the COVID-19 pandemic is on the road to be under control." Indeed, that is the genuine hope that all writers in this volumes hold dearly.

The two chapters by Tai Wei Lim focused on the impact of COVID-19 coronavirus on the global maritime trading route. The first of these two chapters examined the positionality of BRI in the global maritime trading network and its significance to the Chinese political economy. Beijing has much at stakes to ensure the success of the project for the ultimate date of completion in 2049, the centenary anniversary of the founding of the People's Republic of China (PRC) where the BRI is the centerpiece[2] and President Xi Jinping's most important economic diplomatic project. BRI success can enhance the Chinese Communist Party (CCP)'s legitimacy and also propel Xi's personal legacy into the history books, a feature that has been very important for all rulers of China since the dynastic past. Moving from the BRI to the global perspective, the

[2] Calabrese, John (2020). "China's Maritime Silk Road and the Middle East: Tracking against the Wind," Middle East Institute website, accessed 19 May 2020, available at https://www.mei.edu/publications/chinas-maritime-silk-road-and-middle-east-tacking-against-wind.

last chapter before the conclusion examined the impact of Omicron on maritime shipping from a global perspective. This was the most updated infectious variant at the point of this volume's release. Ultimately, as COVID-19 coronavirus mutates, Omicron is just one of thousands of mutations and more variants will appear likely emerge in the future, and state behavior as well as consumer reactions to these variants will continue to shape the maritime shipping industry. The industry players along with officials needed to calibrate their policies and actions carefully to prevent any crew-change crisis and reversing progress made in restoring global trade and supply chains and to work together to ensure that the impact of crew changes due to omicron is reduced.

Finally, in his critique on deglobalization essentially, Wing-Lok Hung noted that COVID-19 has created a wide range of transnational problems, from issues with global supplies to the disrupted functioning of modern societies. He leaves us with the thought that, if globalization fails to build a better world with the ideal economic efficiency and equity, this will surely strengthen anti-globalization voices in the post-COVID world.

CPSIA information can be obtained
at www.ICGtesting.com
Printed in the USA
JSHW011148300323
39281JS00001B/70

9 789811 253720